Texas Politics in My Rearview Mirror

Waggoner Carr

with

Byron D. Varner

Republic of Texas Press
an imprint of
Wordware Publishing, Inc.

Library of Congress Cataloging-in-Publication Data

Carr, Waggoner.
    Texas politics in my rearview mirror / Waggoner Carr with Byron D.
    Varner.
        p.   cm.
    ISBN 1-55622-314-5
    1. Texas—Politics and government—1951-. —Humor. 2. Carr,
    Waggoner—Humor. I. Varner, Byron D.   II. Title.
    F391.2.C33   1992
    976.4'063'0207—dc20   92-30785
                                                CIP

ISBN 1-55622-314-5
10 9 8 7 6 5 4 3 2
9209

All inquiries for volume purchases of this book should be
addressed to Wordware Publishing, Inc., at the above address.
Telephone inquiries may be made by calling:
(214) 423-0090

CONTENTS

Wrong number! Speaker au naturel. My son
the entrepreneur. Heap big words. Where'd he
get that prescription? Uncle Earl. Bring 'em
back alive. Par for the course. A smashing
debut. Where's the catapult? Snuff said. The
mike was bugged. Kitty loiter. Call of the wild.
Good for what ails you. Your guess is as good as
mine. Mr. Sam.

No, lady, not *that* office. Some reporters never
get it right. Out of the mouths of teens. Slight
detour. Whooo called? How do you spell
thirsty? He didn't say which one I was. Don't
get mad, get even! We've got to stop meeting
like this. Keep an eye on that light. You should
see the one that got away! It won't be so easy
next time. No telling what might be in there!
Oh, no, not another Indian uprising!

Number nine, not fine. We didn't hire this one!
Confession is good for the soul. Short note,
mean temper. Tough love. Who else are you
hiding? A landslide victory too close to call.
Even if we win, we lose. This guy was m-e-a-n!
There ought to be a law! It's payback time.
Freaks of nature defined. We want what's best
for you. They did me wrong, Judge. Snakes
alive!

FOREWORD

Politics is demanding! Constituents are frequently demanding and political life can be frustrating and irritating but, at the same time, satisfying. Political life requires much of the politician, of his family, of his children. They all are subject to public scrutiny, exposure by the media, barbs by the opposition, and dissatisfaction by almost everyone at some time or another. The saving grace is humor!

In his *Texas Politics in My Rearview Mirror*, Waggoner Carr has collected some great humorous stories. Some are generic and some are personal. All are symbolic.

Any politician's life is made more bearable by the imposed humility which the rapier thrust of humor inflicts. Everyone, friend or foe, should get many a chuckle out of Waggoner Carr's personal experiences and his collection of amusing stories that inevitably gather along the political trail.

John B. Connally, Jr.

WHAT'S IT ALL ABOUT?

Nowadays, celebrity status intrigues a lot of people who enjoy getting the lowdown on higher-ups in our society. Many folks are fascinated by those in the limelight and consider such Very Important People to be different from us ordinary folks. Hollywood's distortion of real life in its movie and television portrayals may have something to do with it, as well as our acceptance of glamorized articles in magazines, books, news stories, and gossip columns. Whatever the cause, its effect is that the average person wants to know "what's it like" to be in such positions.

This book opens that door to the inner sanctum of life in the courtroom, congress, and politics through personal dealings with people in high (and low) places—John F. Kennedy, Lyndon Johnson, John Connally, Earl Warren, John Nance Garner, Sam Rayburn, Dolph Briscoe, Allan Shivers, and many others, plus a few sports figures and show-biz types thrown in for good measure. Except for the one serious chapter on JFK, most of these vignettes humorously strip away the veneer to reveal that most "good old boys" put their pants on one leg at a time just like everybody else.

Someone who supposedly knew about such things once said, "Two things a person should never watch being made are hot dogs and law." Perhaps more people have witnessed the Legislature in action than have seen wiener making but neither process is considered to be a spectator sport—unless you're a participant.

Of the twenty million or so Texas inhabitants, only a relatively small number have been inside their capitol building in Austin, and most folks probably can't name the top five state officials. Some couldn't even name their State Senator or Representative. Nevertheless, Texans enjoy the political process, are curious about their elected officials, and seem to consider them as being different from average citizens.

This inside look at Texas political life comes from a man who traveled the rocky road of law practice and local, state, regional, and national politics during five decades of major change in our national culture. Fortunately, during this time, he was fortified by the one element necessary for survival—a good sense of humor.

Waggoner Carr once told me, "As a young boy, there were two things I wanted to be when I grew up. One was the Heavyweight Boxing Champion of the World and the other was the President of the United States. I soon found out I'd never be big enough to accomplish the former and a funny thing happened to me on the way to the latter—I lost my races for both Governor and Senator."

Growing up in the south plains of the Texas panhandle, young Carr learned perseverance, independence, conservatism, and reverence for God and country. His youth activities revolved around church and the Boy Scouts.

As a student at Lubbock High School during the great economic depression and the terrible dust bowl days of the 1930s, he learned that humor could help ease the hardships of life. He also honed his public speaking skill, an aptitude displayed as a small child when he and younger brother Warlick played games pretending they were ministers and took turns "preaching sermons" to each other on their front porch. Both became members of the high school debate team, winning honors around the state. Later, as students at Texas Tech, they became collegiate debating champions of the southern U.S. region.

During his junior year at Tech, Waggoner met and fell in love with Ernestine Story, a beautiful young coed from Wylie, Texas, north of Dallas. They were married the following year in December 1941.

Public speaking success and a deep interest in government and politics led Waggoner to study law at the University of Texas, a quest that was interrupted by service in the Air Force during World War II. He completed law school after the war and established his Lubbock law practice in 1946.

In 1947 Carr became Assistant District Attorney and one year later won election to Lubbock County Attorney. He continued up the political ladder by winning the 1951 race for State Representative and served in that office for ten years, the last four as Speaker of the House. He distinguished himself as Texas Attorney General from 1963-67, earning recognition of his peers as being the outstanding Attorney General in the nation.

Following unsuccessful bids for the office of Governor and U.S. Senator, Waggoner turned to private law practice in Austin, trying important cases throughout the country and in the Supreme Court. He gave of his talents in other ways through the years, including service as Regent, Texas Tech University; Texas State Commander, American Legion; President, Texas-13 Tax Reform; and Chairman, Action for Metropolitan Government—a study and recommendation for consolidating agencies serving both Travis County and the City of Austin.

Why this book? As a former Lubbock resident, I followed Waggoner Carr's political career with interest through the years. I admire his accomplishments, his unpretentiousness, his quick mind, and his keen sense of humor. We were having lunch together in Austin one day in 1990, when our conversation evolved to a family history I had written. He said he had never written his memoirs, as such, but had recorded many favorite remembrances of his long and interesting political career as a memento for his family. After reading them, I thought they should be shared with the public and persuaded Waggoner to let me edit them and put them in book form. This little volume is the result.

"Truth is stranger than fiction," wrote Lord Byron. Sometimes it is funnier, too, and harder to believe. Dealing with people from all walks of life and from all Texas cultures has endowed Waggoner Carr with a storehouse of wit and wisdom which he now shares in part with you. He seems to enjoy poking fun at himself in these personal vignettes and, in so doing, minimizes his many talents and accomplishments. Those could fill a much larger book . . . but that is another story.

This one looks mostly at the funny and unusual side of Texas law practice, courtrooms, and politics.

Byron D. Varner

☆ PRACTICING FOR ☆
POLITICS

WHAT'S THAT KNOCKING?

Before I became a proficient member of the Lubbock High School Debate Team, I had great difficulty speaking before an audience. I complained to debate coach J. W. Reid that every time I stood to speak my knees shook and my mind stopped working. He broke the spell by saying, "As long as your knees shake and knock together there is nothing to fret about. When they start missing each other, you can begin to worry."

COMIC RELIEF

I worked at various part-time jobs in Lubbock to earn expenses while attending Texas Tech. The one I liked best was ushering at the Palace Theater. The pay wasn't great, but the hours were flexible, I saw every movie free, and it provided some humor and diversion from the difficult economic conditions of those depression days.

Patrons coming into the theater from the bright outside sunshine had difficulty adjusting their eyes to the dark interior. On such an afternoon, I ushered a man to his seat who carried a brim-full sack of popcorn. He followed behind as I led him to the row where he was to be seated. Unable to see clearly and despite my aid, he missed the seat and sat down with some force in the middle of the aisle, spraying popcorn like a geyser all over the adjoining patrons. I helped him to his feet and he groped his way to an isolated seat.

During one Christmas season, a local hardware store set up a full-size Santa Claus in the theater lobby as an advertising gimmick. I spoke as "Santa's voice" through a microphone from an adjacent room, where I could look through a peephole unobserved and see both Santa and the people entering the lobby.

Most of them accepted and enjoyed the charade, but one inquisitive fellow didn't stop at that. He knew I was somewhere nearby because Santa told him the color of his tie, his hair, and other personal tidbits to imply Santa was "live." The man scanned the lobby area for a clue to where I might be until he spied the peephole, which he covered with his hand so I couldn't see.

To keep him from thinking he had found the secret, I asked, "What are you doing over there with your hand against the wall? You look mighty silly." He withdrew his hand as if the wall was suddenly hot, grinned foolishly, and disappeared into the auditorium.

CANDIDATE WHO?

My friendship with Ralph Brock dated back to our Boy Scout days. Returning to Lubbock after passing the Texas Bar exam, he entered the race for State Representative from the Lubbock area that included several of the surrounding counties. My schedule at Tech was such that I volunteered to help him whenever I could.

Among other things, he asked me to accompany him on trips to rallies and campaign speeches at various places in the district. Typical of these visits was a stop in the small town of Seagraves. Ralph parked his old Plymouth car in front of the Black Cat Cafe. He placed a loudspeaker on the roof rack atop his car and connected its long wire to the jukebox inside the cafe. Then he put nickels into the jukebox and held the microphone next to the speaker.

The loud music echoed throughout downtown Seagraves. When each record ended, he announced through the microphone, "Watch the front door of the Black Cat Cafe. Your next representative to the State Legislature, Ralph Brock, will be coming out of there pretty soon to talk with you." After two or three songs, Ralph went out the front door and gave a speech to those gathered around the car.

On election eve, he planned to appear at a rally for all candidates at a city park in Lubbock. Rain fell all that day and Ralph thought there would be little or no turnout for the Lubbock gathering and decided instead to go to another rally in the small town of Tokio. He asked me to stay and speak in his behalf if anyone did come to the park. Soon after he left town, the sky began to clear and a large crowd assembled at the appointed hour for the Lubbock rally. So many candidates came be seen and heard that the coordinators had to limit each speech to two minutes.

The program chairman introduced me when Ralph's time came and I opened with a funny story. It got such good reaction that I expanded it a bit and gave the punch line just as the bell rang. There was no time left to say anything about Ralph or his candidacy.

Ralph lost by a very narrow margin and when I got the courage to tell him what happened, he reprimanded me with, "My gosh, Waggoner, I believe if you had just mentioned my name I might have won this race!"

A LESSON THAT STUCK

While at Texas Tech, I majored in government as part of my prelaw studies. I also entered the race for Student Business Manager and printed some campaign stickers to put on car bumpers around the campus. Unfortunately, I stuck one on my history professor's car. When he returned and saw the sticker, he was infuriated. Shortly afterward, he spotted me putting stickers on other cars, slowed down as he passed by, and stared a hole right through me. I learned then not to put stickers on any cars without permission. What's more, I lost the race to an *agriculture* major!

WE CHARGE FOR ADVICE!

After his financial struggle to get through law school, friend Dudley Brummett looked forward to making a lot of money from his newly established Lubbock law practice. However, it was quite some time before the first client found Dudley's low-rent office.

The man had marital problems and wanted to know what his legal rights were in dividing property with his wife. Dudley wasn't sure what advice to give, but didn't want to lose his first and only client, so he convinced the man to come back in two days for a conference.

Brummett went to great lengths researching the law and writing a thorough legal brief, which he read aloud to the client at their meeting. Understanding little of it, the client accepted the copy, shook Dudley's hand, and thanked him for the help. On the way out, he noticed the wall sign given to all new attorneys by the Lubbock Bar Association. It read: "We Charge for Advice."

The client returned to Dudley's desk and asked how much he owed him. Unaware of the going rate for legal fees and somewhat surprised by his client's question, the naive attorney said, without thinking, "Oh, six bits will be okay." For those not familiar with that monetary sum, Dudley's first "get rich" legal fee amounted to seventy-five cents.

THE DEFENSE RESTS

Early in my law practice I was appointed co-counsel to represent a defendant charged with murder. My co-counsel was as inexperienced as I was and we both knew it. Neither of us had much of a clientele so there was plenty of time to prepare the case. The trial lasted only a couple of days, but it was difficult for us. The District Attorney's final argument to the jury ridiculed our efforts, saying we had never presented any defense to the killing. "What is their defense for this crime?" he repeatedly asked the jury. He bore down so heavily on this that I quietly urged my co-counsel to state our defense when he made his argument.

Facing the jury confidently, he began: "Gentlemen of the jury, I am deeply disappointed by the District Attorney's inability to understand the theory of the defendant's case. We have tried this case for two days and the District Attorney, unfortunately, still does not understand. Of course, I am sure the members of the jury have no problem understanding it, but for the sake of the District Attorney himself, let me say again what our defense is . . ." and he raised his arm for emphasis . . . then hesitated for a long moment . . . and without stating it, continued . . . "and further-more, let me discuss this point with you!" He concluded his argument and returned to the counsel table. I whispered to him, "What was the matter? You never stated our defense." Somewhat perplexed, he replied, "To tell you the truth, I couldn't think what it was!"

AUTO RECALL

Early in my law practice, I decided that attending a seminar on memory improvement might prove helpful. It was conducted by an out-of-town expert who demonstrated a remarkable memory performance as guest speaker at the local Lion's Club luncheon. He stood in the foyer to meet the members as each one entered the banquet room. Then, as part of his program presentation after the meal, he recalled aloud the name of every individual he met earlier. It was quite impressive to everyone in attendance.

At the end of the two-day seminar, I stopped by my law office to check my telephone calls before going home. As I came out of the building, I saw the memory expert standing on the curb looking up and down the street. Thinking he might need help, I asked if he had a problem. "Oh, it's nothing major," he said, "I just forgot where I parked my car."

$25 REWARD

Apache Chief Geronimo's only surviving child walked into my office unannounced one day. Robert Geronimo said he was looking for an honest lawyer and that someone had recommended me. He had traveled five hours by bus from the reservation in Mescalaro, near Ruidoso, New Mexico, and had about 90 minutes before his return bus would leave.

Geronimo's purpose was to file a lawsuit in behalf of the Apaches against motion picture companies, newspapers, magazines, comic books, and all others who had portrayed Chief Geronimo as a savage or an outlaw. He explained that the Chief was a hero who dedicated his life to protecting Indians from invasion and crimes of the white people. He insisted that I come to the reservation to interview the elderly Indians who still remembered his father.

Touched by his story, I couldn't resist the urge to visit his people. For two days, I rode with Robert Geronimo through the reservation, talking with members of his tribe. Among many who impressed me was an old squaw with legs so stiff from age that she couldn't bend them. She sat on the bare floor in front of the wood stove in her small run-down shack and told me of her personal acquaintance with her Chief. Another was an aged man who lay on a cot in his shanty, so weak that he had difficulty breathing after each sentence.

We took a crude road up to higher elevations while eerie lightening and thunder punctuated a storm in the surrounding mountains. There, I interviewed a well-educated, middle-aged man who spoke English much better than his fellow Apaches, most of whom talked with me through an interpreter. This Indian remembered a day when he was a small boy playing in front of a teepee with some friends. He recounted this story:

"Geronimo and his braves were away on a hunt. Suddenly, bullets whizzed over his head and his grandfather sprang from nearby to throw his body across the boys to protect them. The whites had attacked and had taken some of the Indians' valuables and two of Chief Geronimo's wives and their children. The troopers left word that Geronimo would not see them again until he surrendered—but he refused and took his braves south of the border to a mountain hideout instead.

"The U.S. Government offered a $25 reward to anyone who would lead Union troops to find Geronimo and his tribesmen. One of the Chief's cousins finally consented. As the troops entered the valley below Geronimo's high perch, where he had positioned his braves for an ambush, the Chief saw his cousin in the lead. He signaled his warriors not to attack and went down to powwow with his cousin. The cousin talked him into surrendering on the government's promise that Geronimo would be reunited with his family and all his tribe and companions would be allowed to live in peace. Instead, they took him prisoner and shipped the tribe by train to Florida swampland and then transferred them to a reservation in Oklahoma, where they imprisoned the Chief. He soon agreed to do whatever the white man wanted, in order to protect his people from further injustices."

The Indian also told me, during another visit to the reservation, this story of how Geronimo died:

"The Chief drove his team of horses to town and bought some staples. The weather was bitterly cold and he bought a jug of whiskey to keep his insides warm. On the way home he became drunk and fell off the wagon into a snow-covered ditch. When his team and wagon returned without him, members of the tribe went to search for him. The next morning, I noticed that there was no smoke coming out of Geronimo's chimney, so I went to investigate. I found Geronimo's wife huddled next to the wood stove with no fire burning. She was too old to realize it. Then I saw Geronimo in the corner of the room with snow and ice on his clothes, but by then I was too late to save him and he died from exposure."

I never did file the lawsuit Robert wanted on the Apache's behalf because I determined through research at the time that Texas law did not protect the memory of the dead.

Later, I met some descendants of Geronimo's cousin. They said the government never paid the $25 reward and they wanted me to collect it along with all the accrued interest—a tidy sum. However, Robert Geronimo took a dim view of my helping collect the cousin's money so I never pursued the matter.

NO OTHER SOUND LIKE IT!

The scene of the crime was in a small one-room dwelling behind the main house on a Lubbock area farm. I went there to investigate the facts surrounding an assault with firearms complaint that occurred during a crap game and talked with a man who said he was a witness to the crime.

The man stated emphatically that the defendant pulled a pistol on the complainant, but I discovered while questioning him that he was not actually present in the room at the time the gun was drawn and exhibited. He was out in the yard relieving himself.

I questioned him further:

Q: "How can you be so sure the accused drew a pistol on the complainant if you didn't see it?"

A: "I know there was a pistol drawn because there's always the same kind of noise when any gun is pulled out in a crowd like there was in that room that night."

Q: "What kind of noise is that?
A: "Like everybody trying to get out of the room at the same time."

☆ CLIMBING THE ☆ POLITICAL LADDER

THE PHOTO WAS WORSE THAN I THOUGHT!

Campaigning was not a totally new experience for me. I had played at it in college and helped friends in the real world of politics, but it was considerably different when I did it the first time for myself, running for Lubbock County Attorney. My law practice was new and my clients were few, so I had ample time—and I was diligent.

First, I ordered a number of printed placards and posters with my picture on them and drove my old car all around the county, tacking posters to every utility pole I could find. Sometimes on very cold days, I'd have to chip ice off the pole before I could attach the posters. Starting at the southwest corner of the county, I crisscrossed every road in the entire area, missing not a one. I kept an accurate map of everywhere I'd been and I stopped at every opportunity to knock on farmhouse doors, meet the voters, and leave my literature.

In the latter days of the campaign, I concentrated on the population within the city of Lubbock, but by that time there were few poles in the county that did not feature my smiling face.

One farmer laughingly told me, "If you get elected, you may not be the best County Attorney Lubbock ever had, but your ugly face will be the best known."

IT DIDN'T WORK LIKE THAT IN TEXAS

In my youth I was attracted to books on political subjects. One I liked very much was *Every Man a King* by Huey Long. In it, the former Louisiana Governor and U.S. Senator described some of his campaign methods, including an effective way to talk with farmers. He purposely waited until after the farmer was in bed, then drove to the house and knocked on the door. He politely explained to the sleepy farmer how important it was for Huey to meet with him before election day and they sat on the porch and talked.

Huey visited one or two farmers on any given night, then went home to bed. By the next day, word would have spread throughout that small rural area that this young Huey Long must be a good man because he worked through the night to talk to everyone he possibly could.

I thought of that ploy when I ran for County Attorney and decided to wake up some farmers. However, I gave it up almost as quickly as I started. Huey forgot to mention in his book that farmers' dogs don't take kindly to strangers in the middle of the night.

CAN YOU HEAR ME OUT THERE?

Television was in its infancy during my first political campaign and although not many homes had TV sets then, I thought it advisable to make a brief TV speech.

The experience was unforgettable. Sitting at a desk in the studio with spotlights almost blinding me, the only thing I could see were the red lights on the TV cameras well beyond the desk.

I was used to a different kind of public speaking, where one projects his voice. Forgetting about the attached microphone, I spoke unnecessarily loud to be sure my voice projected as far as the cameras.

No doubt the viewers wondered why that fool was yelling at them, but I got elected in spite of it.

I'M IN CHARGE HERE

On my very first day as County Attorney, Justice of the Peace Robertson came bouncing into my office to announce that he was performing a marriage next door and needed a witness. I agreed to act as the witness and followed him to a nearby room where a young couple, their parents, and a few friends awaited. Judge Robertson was obviously impressed with his importance as he conducted the service with much ado and, since I was the new kid on the block, he must have added an unusual statement to the ceremony for my benefit. When he said that part of the ritual, "Now, by authority vested in me," he hesitated, looked squarely at me and said, "As you know, I am Justice of the Peace here." I simply nodded in agreement that he was Justice of the Peace and he concluded the ritual.

BAD GAMBLE

For an area with so many churches, it amazed me how many people in Lubbock County sold and consumed illegal booze in the late 1940s. A popular saying of the time was: "People here drink wet and vote dry."

Following repeal of Prohibition in the 1930s, Texas voters decided whether liquor could be sold in their respective counties. The pious "drys" outnumbered the "wets" in most South Plains counties and the "drys" won every election for years. Eventually, newcomers expanded the population in large enough numbers to turn the tide for the "wets," but for at least two decades, Lubbock folks had to drive a hundred miles or more to buy alcoholic beverages in the nearest "wet" county. Bootleggers made a lot of money in the process and I spent a lot of time prosecuting them.

It seemed to me there were as many bootleggers as law abiding citizens. After World War II, many returning GIs entered Texas Tech to complete their education and a few of them supplemented their meager earnings by running booze at night between Lubbock and Amarillo. They were frequently picked up in another county before they got back home. The real problem was the professional bootlegger.

In one case I recall, the judge excused a large number of prospective jurors for various reasons and it became necessary for me to either accept a known bootlegger on the panel or decline him and further delay an already long, drawn out effort trying to get an acceptable jury.

I gambled on a hunch and accepted him. Among the arguments I made to the panel was subtly directed to the bootlegger juror, I thought, emphasizing this opportunity to eliminate one of his competitors. It seemed like a good idea, but it backfired. The panel couldn't agree on a verdict and the trial ended with a hung jury.

SHE GOT MY GOAT

An elderly spinster with a large herd of goats lived on the periphery of MacKenzie State Park, in east Lubbock. Locals knew her as "Goat Annie." She had an unkempt appearance and proved to be quite outspoken.

The winter of 1948 was a severe one with lots of ice and snow. She found it impossible to feed her goats adequately so she let them roam and eat shrubbery in the state park. The authorities warned her to cease and desist, but she wouldn't. Her excuse was that the government was using military aircraft to drop hay to freezing cattle in the Midwest, but they were not providing any relief at all for her starving goats. She thought it only fair to let them roam in the park. This was not acceptable to the authorities and it became my job to prosecute Goat Annie, who wouldn't hire a lawyer to represent her.

She repeatedly interrupted my line of questions, mostly with comments about her concern for my health. She said she noticed I was rather thin and needed some more meat on my bones. Then she told me I should start drinking goat's milk and recommended that I eat dried alfalfa and said she would be more than glad to supply them to me.

The judge and jury seemed to enjoy my difficulty trying to get straight answers from her and it was obvious that her irrelevant personal comments bothered me. What really "got my goat," however, was the jury's acquittal of Goat Annie!

★ ON TO THE ★ LEGISLATURE

THE NAME GAME

Pie suppers were popular ways to raise money and get one's name before the public in rural areas. Candidates had the opportunity to shake hands with voters, make speeches and impress them enough so they would remember their names. I devised a scheme to accomplish this early in my campaign for State Representative. At every event I would begin my speech by saying, "Now, I don't care how you remember my name as long as you remember it. Carr is easy to remember. Just think of Ford car . . . little car . . . big car . . . etc."

This unique approach impressed Vernon Townes, candidate for Terry County Attorney in nearby Brownfield. I was late arriving at a pie supper held in my Legislative district and when I got there, Vernon was speaking to them on his behalf. He was saying, "Don't forget my name, folks, it's easy to remember. Just think of big towns, little towns, country towns, etc." His eyes got as big as half-dollars when he recognized my face in the crowd of those listening to his plagiarizing my words.

I'LL NEVER FORGET OLD WHAT'S-HIS-NAME

I covered the counties of my district like a blanket when I ran for the State Legislature and met a lot of people. My name was quite well known, I felt sure. On the day following my election, I was driving around Lubbock with my car radio tuned to a man-on-the-street program originating from the nearby town of Levelland. The host asked questions of people passing by and rewarded them with tickets to a local theater if they answered correctly.

To my surprise, one of the questions was "Who is Waggoner Carr?" I thought it was quite an easy question, but the contestant was slow to answer. Then, after what seemed a long period of silence, he said, brightly, "Oh yeah, didn't he die last week or something?"

WAS THAT A RHETORICAL QUESTION?

Sidewalk interviews remind me of the emcee who asked a passing pedestrian, "Sir, some people say that one of the biggest problems in America today is ignorance and apathy. What would you say to that?

Somewhat irritated, the man snapped, "I don't know and I don't care!"

A DOGGONE SHAME

I'm not aware that a similar bill ever passed the Texas House since my days there, but one of my first official acts as a freshman legislator was to introduce my infamous "dog bill," fulfilling a promise to my postman during the campaign.

The bill placed liability on owners for damages caused when their dogs attacked postal carriers without provocation. Such attacks were a significant problem in Lubbock at the time. When the bill was placed on the calendar for debate, I stood to explain it to the House members. Completing my remarks, I noticed several of them lined up at the microphone to discuss the bill or propose amendments to it.

The first one asked, "Does your bill apply equally to ordinary dogs and show dogs? If not, I may make an amendment to that effect." I patiently explained that it applied to all dogs.

Another wanted to know "Will your bill apply to any dog within ten feet of a fireplug?" I said that it would. I could sense the rest of the members were warming to the occasion. By the end of the following question, I realized there was little possibility for any serious acceptance of my bill and that I was being laughed out of court.

"Mr. Carr," the member intoned, "I'm thinking of proposing an amendment to your bill, but I would like to get your reaction to this proposal before I present it.

It would provide that your bill would not apply to any country dog that was in town for purely sociable purposes. What do you think?"

I thought I'd forget the dog bill.

YOU GOTTA OBEY THE LAW

The Balinese Room was a well-known Galveston gambling casino located on a pier extending some distance out over the water. The proprietors installed an electronic lock on the door within the long hall leading from the beach to the dining/gambling room. As a member of the House Committee investigating organized crime, I conducted hearings on gambling in Galveston. One witness was the Galveston County Sheriff. The following was part of our dialogue during the cross-examination:

Q: "Sheriff, you have told us in detail about how you have cleaned up crime in Galveston County. You described the way you closed houses of ill repute and similar crime centers, but you failed to mention the Balinese Room. Will you tell me whether you've ever attempted to raid the Balinese Room to stop the gambling there?

A: "Yes sir, I've tried to raid that place several times, but have not been successful."

Q: "Can you tell us what happened on those occasions?"

A: "Well, Sir, I get my men together and we go down there to raid that place. The doorman sees us drive up and says to me, 'Why, Sheriff, what are you doing here?' I tell him we are here to raid this place. He always says, 'Sheriff, you know the laws of this state and to come to this place you need to be a member, since it's a private club. Are you a member of the Balinese Room?' I have to tell him I am not a member. He always says, 'Well, then, Sheriff, you've got to obey the law and I can't let you in since you are not a member.' There is nothing left for me to do, Mr. Carr, but take my men back to the station."

I'VE GOT Y'ALL COVERED!

Criminals thwarted several attempts by the Texas Rangers to successfully raid the Balinese Room. By the time lawmen broke through the electronic door and made the long hallway approach to the gaming room, management had eliminated the appearance of gambling and patrons seemed to be dining casually with no evidence to the contrary.

Things went differently on one occasion, however. One of the Rangers gained access to the attic above the dining room. At a preset time, Rangers were to break through the electronic door and the attic Ranger was to drop down into the room and hold everyone at bay until the main force arrived.

The attic Ranger made his move exactly when the second hand reached the appointed hour. What was not planned was his accidental step through the rafters causing him to crash through the ceiling of the Balinese Room. Even worse, his foot caught on a rafter and he was suspended upside-down in midair directly over the crap table. Before the startled occupants could react, the fast-thinking lawman reached up, drew down his pistol and yelled, "DON'T NOBODY MOVE!!!" Everyone "froze" in place.

BLOND BOMBSHELL

Another crime committee hearing resulted when the Waco Junior Chamber of Commerce requested that we investigate the bawdy houses on the outskirts of that city. The Jaycees suspected criminals were paying county law enforcement officials to allow the operations to continue.

Texas Rangers prepared a number of subpoenas for the hearing. The main target was the women who supposedly worked in those houses, but the news leaked out and they could serve only one subpoena. Nevertheless, we held our scheduled meeting at the Capitol Building in Austin and the lone witness appeared.

The committee sat on one side of a table and the witness faced us from the other side. Behind the witness were chairs for the media representatives and the public. I was about three feet from the witness during my questioning.

She was a petite blond, skilled in the art of answering incriminating questions. Her memory was phenomenal. She could easily recall everything she wanted to but couldn't remember anything that would incriminate her or others. I asked her repeatedly about various aspects of the operation, but to no avail. Finally, thinking a complete change of pace might throw her off, I paused, adjusted my eye glasses, and nonchalantly asked, "Is your hair naturally blond?"

Like a shot, she jumped up from her seat, leaned as far as she could across the table into my face, and shouted, "What do you think, you four-eyed son of a bitch?"

DON'T TELL HIM I'M THAT S.O.B.

The Waco hearing reminds me of when I campaigned for my second term in the Legislature and knocked on the door of a farmhouse. I introduced myself and handed the farmer my brochure, saying I would appreciate his vote.

He responded enthusiastically, "Well, you certainly have my vote, young man. I want anybody in there except that S.O.B. who is there right now!"

LET ME REPHRASE THAT

The crime committee also held a hearing at Houston's Rice Hotel, at a time when that city was referred to as the "murder capital of the nation." The mayor, chief of police, and various law enforcement officials testified dramatically about their good efforts in holding down crime. Their testimonies didn't agree with our research, however, so I asked them to take the committee members to some of these "cleaned-up" crime areas so we could see the results of their efforts.

That evening we rode in patrol cars to various sites and the press corps followed in their own vehicles. We stopped first at what was described as a former brothel where the "madam" obviously expected us. She was very courteous and answered all questions as she showed us the premises—luxuriously furnished, thickly carpeted, and with a large display of expensive art. It seemed deserted. As we got back into our cars, she called sweetly, "Y'all come back sometime, ya hear?"

There was no visible evidence of liquor at any of the night spots we visited. I felt sure they were expecting us and had cooperated with the officials until we left town, but I couldn't prove it. Finally, about midnight, the patrol cars delivered us to our hotel. One reporter asked me what I thought about crime in Houston. Upset that the local authorities thought we would believe what they showed us on their apparently contrived tour, I complained sarcastically, "From the crime I've seen tonight, I would say there is more crime in Pyote, Texas, than there is in Houston, Texas."

Pyote is a small West Texas town that was the site of a large Army Air Force base during WW II. The government closed the base after the war, eliminating most of Pyote's population and its claim to fame. I knew absolutely nothing about crime in Pyote and I'd have been surprised if there was any. The name just popped into my head.

The next morning, I read the *Houston Chronicle's* bold headline: "**More Crime In Pyote Than In Houston, Investigator Says.**"

Shortly afterwards, the hot-under-the-collar mayor of Pyote called me and wanted to know "What in hell do you know about crime in Pyote, Texas?"

THAT WAS THEN, THIS IS NOW

The multimillion dollar illicit liquor traffic syndicate in West Texas was another crime group the members of the House Committee investigated. To give witnesses as little advance notice as possible before the hearing started on Monday, I instructed the Texas Rangers to serve subpoenas just two days before—on Saturday.

Among those subpoenaed witnesses was a bootlegger from Snyder. Research convinced me he was the key witness because the syndicate required all other bootleggers to purchase their supply from him. I decided to call him as my first witness. My reasoning for this was that he wouldn't be accustomed to the bright lights, cameras, and microphones in the hearing room at first and might respond to my questions in that setting better than he would later on in a more subdued atmosphere. The cross-examination dialogue went like this:

Q: "What is your name?"
A: "I refuse to answer that question on the grounds that it might incriminate me."

Q: "You are a bootlegger in Snyder, Texas, aren't you?"
A: "No, sir."

Q: "Now look here, I have this thick file on you. I know every long-distance telephone call you've made for the past two years. I know everywhere you've been. I have dates, times, and places. By Texas law, if you lie while under oath, you commit perjury. Perjury here is a penitentiary offense. If you lie to this committee, we are determined to send you to prison. Do you understand this?"

A: "Yes, sir."

Q: "All right then. Let's wipe the record clean and I will ask you these questions again. Are you a bootlegger in Snyder, Texas?"

A: "No, sir."

Q: "You mean to tell me that you are not a bootlegger in Snyder, Texas?"

A: "Yes, sir, I am not."

Q: "Well, then, when did you quit?"

A: "Last Saturday."

NAME DROPPER!

Price Daniel was Attorney General of Texas during my tenure in the Legislature. I invited him to come to my area of the state and let me arrange a tour in anticipation of his running for higher office in the future. He agreed.

For three days we followed a rigid schedule throughout that West Texas district until we both were weary to the point of dullness. The final event was a banquet arranged by the Chamber of Commerce in Morton, a small county seat near the New Mexico border. Having both the Attorney General and their State Representative present at the same time was a big occasion in Morton and they put a lot of work and planning into the event, decorating the tables with candles and making it a high society affair.

I was proud to have such a high ranking state official as my friend and guest on this occasion. As a relatively new Legislator, I thought his appearance would help both my district and my political future. I praised him highly in my introductory remarks, heavily emphasizing our close personal friendship.

He stood up to make his address and received loud and sustained applause. My big smile turned to a stunned look in a matter of seconds, however, when he opened with, "It is indeed an honor for me to be here in this district represented by my wonderful friend, Representative Waggonseller."

HE JUST BLEW INTO TOWN

Wharton Representative Jack Fisk stopped for an unexpected visit with me in my Lubbock office while passing through town. Somewhere between Muleshoe and Lubbock, he saw what he thought was a tornado hit the ground some distance away and move in his direction.

He stepped on the gas to try and outdistance it, repeatedly glancing over his shoulder to make sure he was gaining on it, when suddenly a large whirlwind moved across the road ahead. Not knowing the difference in a whirlwind and a tornado, he tried to stop, but couldn't, and passed through the tail of it . . . shaken but unharmed. Somewhat relieved to have come through the encounter safely, Jack declared: "The only thing I learned from the experience was that it don't do much good to put your brakes on going 120 mph!"

I'LL DRINK TO THAT!

Another of my comembers in the House was an elderly, and often inebriated, gentleman from the northeast section of the state. As time and tension grew during the session, he imbibed in strong drink to the point of public intoxication. When word of this drifted back to his district and the next election rolled around, he faced a female opponent who made it her major campaign issue.

The biggest rally of the campaign took place on the eve of the election and his opponent spoke first, playing on his drinking habits by emphasizing the word "sober" throughout her remarks. She said when voters elected her State Representative she would fulfill her duties in a sober manner, with proper sober reflection and she would at all times be in a proper sober state of mind to do the best job possible. She continued along this hard line throughout her speech.

The incumbent began his address by saying, "I have just heard my lady opponent's speech and I am impressed, as I know you are, by the fact that she is going to stop drinking."

☆ MISTER SPEAKER ☆

WRONG NUMBER!

Allan Shivers served as Texas Governor longer than any other person in history. This strong leader gained a number of political enemies during his career, but on this special day, friends and foes alike gathered to hear his final State of the State address before a joint session of the Texas Legislature. It also was one of my first duties as the newly elected Speaker of the House to preside over the session.

Members of the House and Senate brought families and guests and the House balcony was filled to overflowing with interested citizens. Representatives of press, radio, and television strung endless wires and attached a glut of microphones to the podium.

At the appropriate time, I rapped the gavel for order and announced the entrance of Governor Shivers and his party. They ascended onto the platform and filled every chair, including mine. After I introduced the governor and he came to the podium, I found it necessary to walk to the far corner of the platform to take the seat he had occupied.

The crowd was at rapt attention as the governor reached the climax of his address when, like a bolt out of the blue, one of the podium telephones rang! Since I had to cross the platform to reach the instrument attached to the lower part of the podium, I remained seated, hoping it wouldn't ring again. It did, and seemed even louder and more distracting than the first time. The governor gave me a sidelong glance as if to say, "If you don't answer it, I'm going to!"

On the third ring, I walked in a half-crouching manner and kneeled at his left knee to answer the call. The eyes of the audience, the TV cameras, and the governor were on me as I picked up the handset. I half mumbled, half whispered a reply, quickly hung up and returned to my seat as inconspicuously as possible. The governor later told me that was the most publicized telephone call in the history of Texas.

Who had called? My wife! Unaware of what was going on in the House chamber, she wanted to know if I'd invited any dinner guests for that evening.

SPEAKER AU NATUREL

A long hall at the rear of the House Chamber led to the Speaker's office, other offices, public telephones, and the Speaker's apartment. House members, their secretaries, and guests crowded the hall when the Legislature was in session. There was a metal plate sign on the Speaker's apartment door to identify those quarters, but the general public sometimes paid no attention to the sign and just walked in unannounced if the door was not locked.

After a long day of presiding, early in my first term as Speaker, I was sitting alone in the apartment enjoying some much needed relaxation. I had stripped down to my undershorts, was having a cool drink and watching television, when I was startled by the sound of strange voices. Some public visitors obviously had entered the apartment and were headed my way. I quickly crouched behind the largest chair, hoping for the best and trying to think of something witty to say in my defense.

Fortunately for me, the uninvited guests only paused a moment and continued on their way. Unfortunately for them, they missed what could have been the highlight of their tour.

MY SON THE ENTREPRENEUR

When I became Speaker, son David was eight years old and a very enterprising lad. He quickly adjusted to the "fish bowl" environment of our quarters and the activity around us. I didn't realize how much, however, until he started some activity of his own.

I had taken a brief respite from the Speaker's duties and was walking toward the apartment when, to my amazement, I saw David at the entry door with home-made signs advertising lemonade, fortune telling, and tours at ten cents each.

Neither Mrs. Carr nor I was aware of David's planned lemonade and fortune telling business until he set up shop there, nor that his tour included our apartment—until we intercepted his entourage of House members and guests coming through our living room.

HEAP BIG WORDS

I always prided myself on speaking well in front of crowds, especially when it was a patriotic theme. Something about it starts my adrenalin flowing. One such occasion for me was a July Fourth celebration in Belton.

It was a typically hot Central Texas summer day that required frequent mopping of brows. The large crowd assembled there was exceptionally receptive to my remarks and the frequency and sound of their applause increased steadily as I went along. Their response bolstered my confidence and propelled my own enthusiasm to greater heights. The climax came near the end of the speech where I was supposed to say (with all the vim, vigor, and arm waving I could muster), "You red-blooded Americans must not tolerate the actions of those who would destroy our American heritage."

Much to my dismay, the words came out: "You full-blooded red Americans." Realizing my obvious mistake, I quickly restated the intended phrase and it came out "You full-blooded red Americans" again! Rather than try it the third time, I simply continued where I left off, finished the speech and sat down.

An elderly gentleman hobbled up to me afterwards, shook hands, complimented me on my speech, and then added:

"It's too bad there weren't any Indians here to appreciate it."

WHERE'D HE GET THAT PRESCRIPTION?

Until Lyndon Johnson became vice president, only one other Texan had ever held that office. John Nance Garner was elected as Franklin Roosevelt's running mate in 1933 and held the office eight years. He later appraised the job as not being worth "a warm bucket of spit." The crusty old politician retired to his home in Uvalde.

Governor Dolph Briscoe was a State Representative from Uvalde when I was Speaker of the House. I had always wanted to meet John Garner and I asked Dolph if he could arrange a visit sometime. He said he'd try. Not long after that, Dolph called and said we could see the famous "Cactus Jack" on the following Sunday morning.

Mr. Garner had donated his main house to the historical society and was living in a smaller one behind it. We arrived about midmorning and found him seated at a large round oak dining table, dressed in a khaki shirt and khaki trousers with a large black unbuckled leather belt. He was reading the *Houston Chronicle* when he looked up at us and said profanely, "If this damned paper gets any bigger, I'm gonna have to quit reading it."

As we visited, he told stories about himself and President Roosevelt. I was fascinated. Without realizing it, I said from time to time, "You don't say," or "Is that the truth?"

Finally, Mr. Garner stopped his story and said, "Young man, you don't have to ask me if I'm telling you the truth. You're damned right I am telling you the truth!"

An hour or so later, he took his watch out of his pocket and announced, "Gentlemen, it's time for my medicine. Come join me." Too polite to ignore an obvious command, Dolph and I followed him to the kitchen where he took a chipped pitcher from the refrigerator, got an old peanut butter jar from the shelf, and then reached for his medicine—a fifth of bourbon. He poured a generous portion of the whiskey in the jar and handed it to me. Frankly, I didn't know if I could down it without choking, especially on Sunday morning. I had little alternative, however, so I held my breath and swallowed it. I was almost afraid to breathe until he poured some water in the same jar and instructed me to drink it. He poured a like amount in the jar for Dolph, who found it as difficult as I had. Finally, he completed the cycle with a strong "dose of medicine" for himself and we returned to the oak table for more conversation.

It was still before noon when the three of us returned to the kitchen for our second dose—same jar, same medicine. By then I was beginning to feel pretty good and thought this stuff might be curative after all.

Mr. Garner told us a few more stories until his housekeeper interrupted to remind him it was time for his nap. As if turning off a light, he got up, thanked us for our visit, and left the room. We stood there for a brief time savoring the moment and departed.

UNCLE EARL

Louisiana Governor Earl Long was noted for being somewhat uncouth, unpredictable, and profane. Towards the end of his final term, he telephoned me wanting to know the whereabouts of Texas Governor Price Daniel. I told him I hadn't seen the governor that day. He started ranting about how terrible it was that the Texas Governor had not been available to greet him because "I always greet visiting governors when they come to Louisiana." I replied that Governor Daniel probably didn't know that Governor Long was in the state. Long said he was in Fort Worth for the evening and was heading out the next morning to visit a girl-friend in Abilene. Before he hung up, he made me promise to get in touch with Governor Daniel and "teach him some manners."

On an airline flight sometime later, I sat next to Senator Russell Long, Earl's nephew, and related the incident to him. By then, Uncle Earl was acting even more peculiar, wearing sacks over his head and doing other outrageous things until they confined him to a rest home. Senator Long expressed no surprise about his uncle's call to me and said, "My Uncle Earl is the damndest fellow."

Governor Long had a good political friend in his Attorney General Jack Gremillion, but somewhere along the way Jack got tired of the governor's odd activities and broke with him. Earl used every opportunity to get back at Gremillion. His favorite saying was, "If you want to hide anything from my Attorney General, put it in a law book."

BRING 'EM BACK ALIVE

Speakers sometimes have problems maintaining a quorum of members present to properly conduct the business of the House. Members leave for a variety of reasons, such as an intent to break a quorum and prevent voting on a bill, or simply because they've had enough for one day.

During one evening session, a member made a point of order that a quorum was not present and the roll call confirmed it. The House voted to put a "call to the House," which meant I had to send the sergeant-at-arms and his assistants to "arrest" the missing members, bring them back, and confine them behind locked doors to prevent their "escape"—until they completed the House business.

One assistant sergeant-at-arms was a tall, muscular law student, physically capable of doing his job with ease. After the session I learned about his confrontation with a burley Dallas area Representative, Ben Atwell. Ben's nickname was "Jumbo." The assistant traced him to a prominent motel on South Congress Avenue and knocked on the door. Atwell was older, but equally big and tough looking. He refused to leave at first. But, having been a law student himself, he relented when the assistant said, "Please, Mr. Atwell, don't make me physically force you to come back to the Capitol. That will make me lose my job and I need it to help me finish law school. But, the Speaker told me to bring you in and I aim to do it any way I have to!"

PAR FOR THE COURSE

It is difficult for golfers to resist when the game beckons on a beautiful sun-filled afternoon in Austin. On such a day, one of my committees was in public session debating some important and controversial bills before a large crowd of witnesses and visitors. I walked through the House chamber and happened to look through a window on the south side of the Capitol. There on the street below were three of my top legislative leaders putting golf clubs in the car, preparing to drive away. Impulsively, I opened the window and shouted, "Hey, you S.O.B.s, get back up here and do your work!" Then, I realized that everyone in the chamber heard this loud outburst even clearer than the would-be golfers had. The truants did return although, as it turned out, there was a quorum without them.

A SMASHING DEBUT

It is a long-standing tradition of the House Speaker to invite various members to preside in brief stints. It gives them additional legislative experience, a feel for the responsibility of the office, and, if they happen to have constituents sitting in the balcony, a certain amount of prestige.

On the podium was a steel plate to hit the gavel against. It made a sharp noise and was the Speaker's sound of authority when he banged the instrument down.

I once signaled Midland Representative Andy Anderson to provide such service for me while I took a short break in the Speaker's office. Through a small speaker on my desk I heard Anderson call for a vote and, when it ended, he brought the gavel down to signify the voting was to be tabulated.

In his nervousness, Andy missed the steel plate he was supposed to hit and crashed the gavel into the plate glass atop the podium, instead. It caused an ominous shattering noise that was surpassed only by the sound of all the wild laughter it evoked.

Embarrassed but determined, the temporary Speaker again announced the vote and banged the gavel down forcefully—on the proper target this time —and received a standing ovation for his effort.

WHERE'S THE CATAPULT?

My mother had flown very little in her lifetime when she accompanied me on a short campaign trip to northeast Texas in a private twin-engine plane. Our first stop in Longview was for a brief reception and then we returned to the airport to depart for the next town on the itinerary.

Our pilot always stopped on the taxi strip, about 75 feet short of the runway, to check the engines before takeoff. Not aware of this procedure, mother thought we were ready to go but all she could see out her window was the short strip of taxiway we were sitting on.

She looked over at me in wonderment and commented, "My, they certainly are making runways short these days."

SNUFF SAID

Jerry Sadler represented his East Texas constituency in the House. Foes of this former Railroad Commissioner found him to be a tough political opponent. He was also a snuff dipper and kept a spittoon by his desk. During one hard-fought legislative battle over a tax bill, Sadler proposed an amendment to eliminate levying a small tax on snuff. He addressed his fellow members in words like this:

"Ladies and gentlemen of the House. I appeal to you to eliminate this tax because the burden of its payment will fall upon the elderly and poor of my grand eastern part of the state. These old taxpayers can be credited with building this state and now, in their declining years, all they have left to enjoy themselves beyond the necessities of life is a good dip of snuff! This tax would deny them that pleasure of life."

He made such an emotional appeal that I called upon another member to speak against the amendment. Sadler won, but just barely. The closeness of the vote was attributed by many to the opposing member's rejoinder:

"I have heard the emotional appeal of my fellow member, the Honorable Jerry Sadler. His plea is, indeed, heart rendering and sincere. I am sure he speaks for all snuff dippers in East Texas. In my mind's eye, I can picture that old East Texas snuff dipper who, before taking off in his private airplane, pauses at the end of the runway, rolls his cockpit window down, spits his snuff onto the runway and says, 'God bless Jerry Sadler.'"

THE MIKE WAS BUGGED

Towards the end of the legislative session, when the work days grew longer and more tiresome, members sometimes played jokes on each other to help ease the tension. These antics were a harmless form of relief in such times, so long as the Speaker could keep them under control—and tolerate them in good humor if he was the butt of their joke.

My podium microphone was mounted on an arm that could be extended to bring the microphone close to my face. It was a habit of mine to extend it far enough that I could press my lips against it when I talked. The words seemed more distinct and I didn't have to project my voice as much.

During one particularly long work session, I placed one of the House members in the Speaker's chair to preside over the session while I made a brief visit to the Speaker's quarters. I soon returned, took over the gavel, and moved to the microphone to speak.

When I did, something grabbed my lips and I jumped back, startled. The peals of laughter told me it was another setup, but it took me a moment to realize the insect wasn't real.

Some mischievous member had entwined a plastic spider in the mesh of the microphone, its claw-like feet extending outward. That's what "bit" me.

KITTY LOITER

Although Nocona Representative Tony Fenoglio was an effective member of the Legislature, his practical jokes often became a thorn in the Speaker's side. One time he carried it almost too far.

To start each daily session, I asked the House Chaplain to give an invocation. One morning, just as I started to bow my head, a bizarre sight caught my eye. There atop Tony's desk was what appeared to be a half-grown lion with a chain around its neck, its legs sprawled in all directions.

The situation so distracted me that I hardly heard what the chaplain was saying and when he finished, I called the sergeant-at-arms to approach the podium. "Do you see what I see on Fenoglio's desk?" I asked in disbelief. He turned in that direction and answered, "It looks like a lion to me!"

"Well, go over there right this minute," I ordered, "and tell him I said to get that thing out of here!" Trying to continue my duties with composure, I kept glancing Tony's way until I saw him acknowledge my message, pull the lion off his desk by its chain, and nonchalantly lead it out of the chamber, as if it were an ordinary household pet.

CALL OF THE WILD

Most Legislators liked to hunt and fish, including my friend and fellow member Max Smith, who represented San Marcos. A curious thing happened one day while we hunted deer together in the hills west of San Antonio.

Max was in his deer blind when he shot and hit a nice buck, but it ran into the nearby brush. He got out of the blind and ran after the deer before it got away. When he approached the spot, the deer charged toward him and Max grabbed it by the antlers, wrestled it to the ground, and finished the job with his hunting knife.

When Max stood up, he noticed in disbelief that the buck he thought he had wounded was lying dead in the bushes a few feet away.

He had killed a fresh deer a la Daniel Boone.

GOOD FOR WHAT AILS YOU

Bill Blakeley was an influential Texan during his time. He was wealthy, owned a large Texas ranch, was president of Braniff Airlines, and filled the appointed U.S. Senate seat created by the resignation of Lyndon B. Johnson to become vice president.

My own introduction to Senator Blakeley was a chance meeting at Austin's municipal airport, while we waited to board an airliner. We walked from the terminal to the plane together, then sat together for the trip to Dallas.

As we started up the portable stair to board the plane, the hostess greeted us warmly. Much to my surprise, Blakeley pointed to me and said to her, "Young lady, do you know who this is?" She said she didn't. "This gentleman is the Speaker of the Texas House of Representatives!" In her nice way, the hostess said, "I am pleased to meet you, sir."

Not to be outdone, I responded by pointing to him and asking her, "Do you know who this is?" She admitted she didn't know him, either. "Well," I told her, "he owns this airplane." That really got her attention!

In our conversation during the flight, he surprised me by saying, "Waggoner, I've never seen you drunk." Not being that well acquainted with him, and somewhat taken aback by his comment, I merely replied, "That's right, Senator."

"Well," he advised, "you ought to get drunk every once in a while. It's good for a man."

YOUR GUESS IS AS GOOD AS MINE

I never had a good feel for estimating the number of people attending any political gathering. Unless there was some mechanism for an actual count, the number science was mostly a guess. If the rally benefited you or your party, the guess was probably a fat one in your favor. This science was clearly demonstrated to me during the presidential campaign when Democrats John Kennedy and Lyndon Johnson made a brief stop for an airport rally in Lubbock. I was chairman and master of ceremonies.

The crowd was at its peak when the candidates arrived and a local newsman, wanting to file his story as early as possible, ran up to me and asked if I had any idea how many people were there.

I turned to one of the members of the country music band playing for the occasion and asked him, "Hank, you're used to crowds, how many people do you think are here today?" He took a quick glance and responded without hesitation, "7,500." That sounded good to me and I relayed the information to the reporter who raced away to write his story.

MR. SAM

Sam Rayburn was Speaker of the U.S. House of Representatives for a number of years, including my time in the Texas House until I became Speaker, and I was privileged to visit with him on several occasions before then. His outward expression seemed gruff to those who didn't know what a kind and considerate person he really was.

Mr. Sam was suffering from a terminal illness the last time I called him at his home in Bonham. He had taken a brief leave from his Washington duties to go there for a few days rest. I told him I'd like his counsel before I ran for Speaker and he said, "Waggoner, I'm hurting like hell right now and would like to delay our visit until I'm feeling a little better." He died before that visit ever took place.

☆ GENERAL CARR ☆

NO, LADY, NOT *THAT* OFFICE

Candidates should realize that some who attend political functions are not as well versed as others are in the political process, even to know who is running for what office.

In the early days of President Kennedy's administration, when his brother Bobby was U.S. Attorney General, I ran for Texas Attorney General. A nice lady came up to me after one of my campaign speeches in Hearne, Texas, and gushed, "Oh, Mr. Carr, I am so glad you are running and I sure hope you win. I am getting sick and tired of seeing and hearing about that Robert Kennedy!"

SOME REPORTERS NEVER GET IT RIGHT

Knowing the nonpolitical stance of their organization, I was determined that my speech before the

Dallas Rotary Club would not reflect the fact that I was running for Attorney General. Because of the campaign, I wasn't surprised to find a local reporter outside my hotel room as I left for the meeting. I told him I would be pleased to answer all his questions on my next trip to Dallas if he would forgo the interview this time, as this visit was purely nonpolitical. He said he understood and would look forward to it.

Reading the report of my Rotary speech in the next day's edition of his paper, I was amazed by his lead paragraph that said:

"Former Speaker of the House Waggoner Carr was in the city today to deliver a nonpolitical campaign talk to the Rotary Club."

OUT OF THE MOUTHS OF TEENS

You can't always tell about a person's political affiliation just by a brief encounter. About a month after I won the Democratic nomination for Attorney General, I attended a State Bar of Texas convention in Mexico City and happened to enter the hotel elevator at the same time as a Dallas attorney and his two sons. He recognized me immediately and told me how glad he was I won the primary and that I'd make a great Attorney General.

He turned to his sons and said, "Boys, this is our next Attorney General of the State of Texas and I want you to shake his hand!"

The oldest teen clarified the situation quite well for me when he answered his dad, "What do you care? You didn't support him!"

SLIGHT DETOUR

The inaugural parade for the election of Governor John Connally included open convertible rides for all top state office holders, so this was to be the climax to my own election as Attorney General as well. Every politician loves being in the limelight, especially the opportunity to ride in a big parade and wave at constituents.

Ernestine and I both sat high on the rear seat so we could see and be seen along the parade route, which began at about 2nd Street and proceeded north along Congress Avenue to 11th, turned right for a block, then left along the Capitol grounds to the reviewing stand where the inaugural ceremonies would be held. That was the focal point of all activities and camera crews awaited the arrival of each car there to provide live, state-wide TV coverage—the most important event of the day for the politicians!

Huge crowds lined Congress Avenue and followed the last parade units all the way to the Capitol, causing total blockage of the streets in that entire area when the parade was over. Somehow, when our driver turned off Congress Avenue, he inadvertently followed the unit ahead of him, which must not have been a part of the inaugural ceremonies, and didn't turn left at the Capitol grounds.

We were having such a great time laughing, smiling, and waving to the crowds that we didn't notice what happened until we had gone another block or so. When the crowds thinned—and people looked at us like they wondered, "Who are those people in that convertible and why are they waving?"—we realized something was wrong. It was then impossible to get back into the parade, so I told the driver to take us as close as he could to the reviewing stands where we made our way on foot to the reserved seating area.

When I tapped the guard on the shoulder and introduced myself, he said, "Why, Mr. Carr, we were expecting you to arrive by automobile." So was I!

WHOOO CALLED?

Lawyers sometimes use Latin terms to the point that they take it for granted everyone else knows what they are talking about. When I became Attorney General, my secretary had no legal office experience. She performed her job well and made few mistakes but, because of a Latin term, she made one error that we both remember with a smile.

In response to a telephone call from a Mr. Hammond, on behalf of a group wanting to meet with me for a brief discussion, we set a time for the following day. As was my usual procedure, I called the secretary on the office intercom and told her to enter an appointment in the book for "Mr. Hammond, et al." For reasons I didn't understand, she seemed to have an unusual interest in this meeting.

After the group met with me and left the office, she said disappointedly that she didn't see the dead owl. It required several questions and answers between us before we solved the mystery. Unfamiliar with the legal term et al (meaning and other persons) in my intercom message "Mr. Hammond, et al," she thought I said "Mr. Ham and dead owl."

HOW DO YOU SPELL THIRSTY?

Tequila is a well-known drink throughout the nation today, but at one time, it was an unusual and unrecognizable word in some parts of the country.

My top associates and I were in Cleveland, Ohio, attending a conference for the National Association of Attorneys General. Following our noon arrival at the hotel, we went to the dining room for lunch. The waitress asked if we'd like an appetizer and each, in turn, ordered a drink. "And what will you have?" she asked me last.

"I think I'd like a Tequila Sour," I answered.

"How's that again," she queried. I repeated the order.

Readying her pencil and pad, she asked "Would you mind spelling that for me?" I spelled it. Then she asked me to pronounce it one more time. I did that.

She noted what she'd written on her pad and then, with a quizzical look on her face, told me, "Sir, I don't think we have one of them. If we don't, will a tuna salad be okay?"

HE DIDN'T SAY WHICH ONE I WAS

I thought I'd heard every kind of introduction there was until I spoke before a civic club in Vega, Texas, west of Amarillo. The emcee simply said:

"Some people do not need an introduction. Others do not deserve an introduction. I give you Waggoner Carr."

DON'T GET MAD, GET EVEN!

There are also those personal friends who know funny or embarrassing stories about you and love to use them as anecdotes for their introductions. When that occurs, you can't always think quickly enough to turn the tables with a good "put down" of your own.

However, I rose to the occasion at one such event and got even with the friend who was having a good time at my expense. I told this story:

"When my brother Warlick and I were youngsters, we spent a good deal of our summers playing two-man baseball. We located the bases as space allowed and took turns at bat while the other pitched the ball. During one of my times at bat, I connected solidly with the ball and sent it sailing into left field where it happened to hit our family donkey in the head and killed him. My mother saw what happened, came out of the house, and gave me a stern lecture. She told me, 'That jackass will surely come back and haunt you one day, mark my word.'"

Then, I added, "I believe my mother's prophesy has come true tonight!"

WE'VE GOT TO STOP MEETING LIKE THIS

I'm not sure if the saying "familiarity breeds contempt" is an accurate expression or not, but I remember one judge's statement that made me wonder if he was trying to say this in a nice way.

During my four years as Attorney General, I must have tried more varied and important lawsuits defending Texas than any other AG in modern history. It happened that Federal Circuit Court of Appeals Judge John Brown sat on a number of these cases, until he finally chose to make a statement during one of them.

After being recognized by the Court and rising to my feet to present the argument in behalf of the State of Texas, Judge Brown commented, "It has been the experience and pleasure of this Court and this Judge to become acquainted with most of the Attorneys General in this Judicial District, but let me say this for the record: never have we become so intimately acquainted with any of them as we have the present Attorney General of Texas."

KEEP ONE EYE ON THAT LIGHT

Appearing before the U.S. Supreme Court is always a challenge, no matter how well prepared you think you are. It is the top of the mountain and one can't help but think of it on a grand scale—but sometimes, it's the little things that leave a lasting impression.

Billy Sol Estes, tried in Tyler on a criminal charge, appealed the case on the grounds that the judge's allowing television coverage inside the courtroom had violated Estes's Constitutional rights to a fair trial. This challenge had reached the Supreme Court and I defended the case for the state. John Cofer, a prominent criminal attorney in Austin, represented Estes.

Time restrictions on arguments are strictly enforced and when the red light on the podium turns on, it indicates the speaker's time has expired and he or she must promptly cease talking. The light came on during Mr. Cofer's argument, but he continued on for a sentence or two.

It was time to break for lunch anyway, so when that particular light came on, the Chief Justice and all the other Justices rose in unison and walked out of the courtroom, leaving Cofer speaking.

Thereafter, I concluded that when the red light comes on it indicates: "Stop talking and we don't mean maybe!"

YOU SHOULD SEE THE ONE THAT GOT AWAY!

Hunting and fishing are among my favorite ways to ease tension and to enjoy good fellowship with friends and family. No matter how many times you go, there is always something unique about each excursion. A case in point is a quail hunting trip where I took two Attorney General associates—John Stegall and Sam Kelley—to a ranch in South Texas. Neither had done much hunting and both had to borrow shotguns.

Driving a Jeep along the underbrush, we finally flushed a large covey of quail that flew about 100 yards from us before landing. I stopped the Jeep and instructed Sam to walk about 30 feet to my left and for John to walk about the same distance to my right and we walked toward the spot where the birds landed. Along the way, the mesquite bushes were so high that we lost sight of each other. Soon, I heard sounds of many gunshots coming from Sam's side, but nothing from John's side, and he soon came out of the brush and joined up with me. Sam was nowhere in sight, so the two of us returned to the Jeep to wait for him there. We decided he must have found the birds because we saw none.

When Sam finally arrived, he carried by its ears the largest jackrabbit I had ever seen, but no birds. He made no comment as he approached and didn't seem to want to talk about it. I looked for marks on the rabbit where the shots landed, but there were none, and I continued quizzing noncommittal Sam until he finally described his experience:

"While I was walking through the brush I came across this wild pig, I guess it was one of those javelinas I've heard so much about . . . and it scared the hell outta me. I fired at it several times and stung it good enough to make it real mad. Man, that thing started running in circles around me, grunting and snapping its jaws and I kept firing at it and missing until I ran out of shotgun shells. I figured that pig knew it, too, so I grabbed the gun by its barrel and held it like a baseball bat awaiting the pig's next charge from behind the bush where it disappeared.

"When it came, I swung with all my might and cold-cocked him with the gun handle. Only it wasn't the pig I hit, it was this jackrabbit that ran out from the same bush. I knocked that rabbit about 30 feet and splintered the gun butt when I hit a tree on my back-swing."

IT WON'T BE SO EASY NEXT TIME

Ordinarily, I am a better than average shot and can acquit myself very well with a rifle or shotgun on a hunting trip. There was one time during a deer hunt at the King Ranch in South Texas, however, that I embarrassed myself with what seemed just the opposite of my real ability.

The invitation for the hunt came through former District Judge Authur Klein, of Harlingen, and former State Representative Carl Conley, of Raymondville. The driver of the stripped-down touring car with its top removed was foreman of the ranch, who announced at the outset that no one would shoot until the special guest (me) got his deer. I protested, wanting the other guests to shoot along with me, but the foreman said no, it was a ranch rule and that's the way it had to be.

As we drove around the ranch, he pointed out several large bucks and I shot and missed, shot and missed, until the situation became almost intolerable for me. There I was, time after time failing to hit a deer, while the others patiently waited for my luck to change. I was surprised anyone would even talk to me when we stopped to have lunch with the cowboys.

When we started up again, the foreman spotted a beauty lying in the grass. He pointed his finger at the buck and said, "There's a good one." "Where?" I asked, excitedly.

"Right over there by that tree," he said, still pointing. I took a deep breath, aimed carefully, and hit him. Obviously relieved, the foreman congratulated me on such a good shot and said he expected horns to be flying everywhere. Within the hour, everyone had their deer and we returned to camp.

The next year, I asked Judge Klein if he might get me another invitation to hunt on the King Ranch. He said he didn't know but he'd try. When he called back to tell me the good news, he added a comment from the ranch foreman, who told him it was okay to bring me back down, but to "make sure the son of a bitch understands I might not be able to find him one asleep this time."

NO TELLING WHAT'S IN THERE!

Astronaut Gerald Carr, who once held the record of being in space longer than any other American, is not related to me. We did become good friends over the course of time though, and visited in each other's homes. He told me about some of his experiences as commander of Skylab III.

One experiment that intrigued me was a cargo of living creatures they took with them for a test of survival under conditions of weightlessness. Jerry mentioned spiders, mice, fish, and various plants.

The astronauts left Skylab III and its cargo in its orbit and returned to Earth. I asked him, "What is your best guess at what you might find if you could go back and walk in on all those plants and animals?"

"Well, I don't know," he reflected, "but I'll tell you one thing for sure. I would knock before I entered!"

Sometime after this conversation, Skylab III began loosing altitude in its orbit and burned upon reentry into Earth's atmosphere. Jerry later said he was quite disappointed that NASA, despite its effort to devise some method to do so, was unable to return Skylab III to its orbit and continue the experiment.

OH, NO, NOT ANOTHER INDIAN UPRISING!

Mr. Earl Boyd Pierce, General Counsel for the Cherokee Nation, Muskogee, Oklahoma, visited my office one day and said he wanted to resolve a dispute between his Indian nation and Texas that had existed since Sam Houston's forces defeated Santa Ana's Mexican Army in 1836.

It involved title to more than two million acres of East Texas land once occupied by the Cherokees. Pierce told the story of how Santa Ana approached Cherokee leaders and asked them to attack Sam Houston's forces from the north while he attacked from the south to defeat Houston's army. In return for their help, Santa Ana offered to cede the Cherokee territory to that Indian Nation.

Sam Houston somehow learned of Santa Ana's proposal and made a counter offer that, if the Cherokees would not attack and Houston's army defeated Santa Ana, the new Republic of Texas would give the Cherokees the land. Mr. Pierce produced a copy of Houston's handwritten letter to this effect and said the new Republic not only failed to honor the agreement, but eventually drove the Indians from their Texas land into the Oklahoma territory.

Mr. Pierce said the Cherokee Nation still claimed title to the Texas acreage but, with all the development that had taken place, his people knew it wasn't practical to expect Texas to give back the land. He did say, however, that the oil, minerals, and agricultural production there would justify Texas paying the Cherokees for it, maybe not market value, but they were willing to sell the land to Texas for $1.00 per acre. He continued, "Of course, we know that Texas probably wouldn't just give us $2.5 million dollars for nothing, so our Nation would be willing to spend this money to educate all of our children in Texas colleges and universities, so that in the end, Texas would get back every dollar they paid us for the land. If you and Governor Connally can think of a more equitable way to settle this dispute, let us hear from you."

I contacted Governor Connally and told him of the visit. It was decided that my office would brief the legal problems involved and what authority the governor or the Legislature might have to appropriate public money for such purposes. We found in our review that every Constitution of Texas, up until the one current at the time, authorized the Legislature to appropriate public money to pay such claims. The current one did not, however, so that it would have been illegal for the Legislature to do so. I advised Mr. Pierce of this fact and heard nothing further from him. However, a letter arrived from Castroville, Texas, sometime later, under this letterhead:

CHEROKEE NATION OF NORTH AMERICA
Dr. Dayl J. Flournoy, Chief and War Chief

Dr. Flournoy wrote that he had read newspaper accounts of a proposal made to sell the Cherokee land. He claimed that the person I was dealing with had no authority to make such a proposition.

He further declared that the Cherokee Nation would never agree with Texas on that land and concluded with this statement:

"As an Indian, when my National Council tells me to take up arms in defense of my nation, you can be damned sure I will remember Austin, Texas. For your information the United States Department of State recognizes me as the legal head of the Nation. No treaty—no peace."

I called John Connally and told him, "Governor, it looks like we have an Indian war on our hands!"

We never heard from either of them again.

It was my privilege in 1960 to introduce Senator John F. Kennedy to my Lubbock constituents during a presidential campaign stop there.

Vice president Lyndon Johnson offered his congratulations following my 1963 swearing in ceremony as Attorney General.

Vice President, United States of America

President, United States of America

Governor, State of Texas

TEXAS WELCOME DINNER

NOVEMBER 22, 1963, MUNICIPAL AUDITORIUM, AUSTIN, TEXAS

 PROGRAM

Eugene M. Locke, Master of Ceremonies, Chairman, State Democratic Executive Committee

Music by Volunteers from The University of Texas Longhorn Band. Vincent R. DiNino, Director.

Entrance of National and State Official Guests at Head Tables

Invocation by Dr. Robert Tate, Minister of the First Methodist Church of Austin

The National Anthem

Introduction of Members of the State Democratic Executive Committee by Eugene M. Locke

Introduction of Members of the Texas House of Representatives by Speaker Byron Tunnell

Introduction of Members of the Texas Senate by Lieutenant Governor Preston Smith

Introduction of Guests at Head Tables by Eugene M. Locke

Entrance of Governor and Mrs. John Connally

Entrance of Vice President and Mrs. Lyndon B. Johnson

Entrance of President and Mrs. John F. Kennedy

Welcome by Governor Connally

Remarks by Vice President Johnson

Address by President Kennedy

Benediction by the Very Reverend Edward C. Matocha, Chancellor of the Diocese of Texas

LYNDON B. JOHNSON

JOHN F. KENNEDY

JOHN CONNALLY

This Nov. 22nd "Welcome to Austin" for President John F. Kennedy never occurred.

Foreman Dale Malecheck was my sidekick on a trail drive at the **LBJ** ranch.

John Connally and I share a hearty laugh with comedian Jimmy Durante, who campaigned vigorously and humorously for me during my 1966 U.S. Senate race.

Another hard-working campaigner in that 1966 race was teenage son David Carr.

Bob Hope has long supported the Hughen School for Crippled Children in Port Arthur.

Fun-loving American Legionnaires voted me their "#1 Clown."

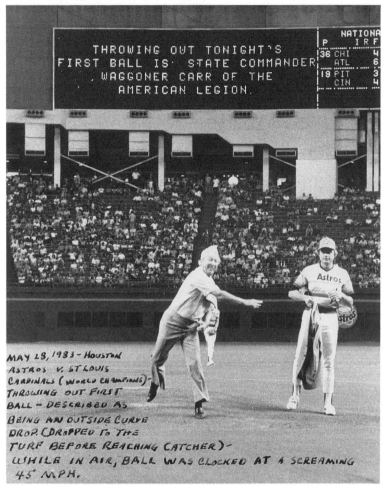

MAY 28, 1983 - HOUSTON
ASTROS V. ST LOUIS
CARDINALS (WORLD CHAMPIONS) -
THROWING OUT FIRST
BALL - DESCRIBED AS
BEING AN OUTSIDE CURVE
DROP. (DROPPED TO THE
TURF BEFORE REACHING CATCHER) -
WHILE IN AIR, BALL WAS CLOCKED AT A SCREAMING
45 MPH.

Baseball was never the same after I threw out (my arm and) the first ball to start a game in the Houston Astrodome. *Astro photo.*

☆ WE GOT LETTERS ☆

Mail to the Attorney General was usually routine, but now and then letters arrived that were unintentionally humorous or eccentric. The following reprints, in whole or part, are typical of those we filed under the heading of "Unusual correspondence." Dates and names are withheld, but each person's grammar, spelling, and punctuation are verbatim.

☆ ☆ ☆

NUMBER NINE, NOT FINE

Texas City, Texas

Dear Sir:

I would like to know my rights under the Texas Election Code in the City election of the City of Texas City.

I, , officially drew position number 8, at the official drawing for the race. My campaign slogan was, "Vote for number eight and get things strait."

On the day of the election, the official ballot had me in position 9-a. This caused me to loose votes.

WE DIDN'T HIRE THIS ONE!

Brenham, Texas

The Attorney General Of Texas

Honorable Sir:

I am a finder I desire to locate gambling places report just ware they are. It a fact that I am a experienced undercover investigator I am said.To be a Ace my reference is with the _____ agency in Dallas, Texas office I know ware seveal placese already.

I will be glad to give your office reports just for finders fee.

My education is high school graduate business school graduate, have a B.S. In criminology and investigator, have a Ps.D.M. In Psychology, Graduate of fingerprint school.

P.S. At this time I am only locate missing persons Skip Tracers

CONFESSION IS GOOD FOR THE SOUL

Texas had a poll tax law requiring a small fee to become a registered voter. The fees helped defray election costs. The U.S. Supreme Court declared this poll tax unconstitutional while I was Texas Attorney General. I received the following letter sometime after the law was changed:

Avinger, Texas

Dear Mr. Carr:

I paid one hundred poll taxes this year or more. Whats more I have been paying them ever year. I have just found out it is agin the law. I aint gonna do it no more, unlessen I have to.

Your Democrat friend.

P.S. I also deliver these votes.

SHORT NOTE, MEAN TEMPER

I had no idea what prompted this brief message, but to emphasize his obvious displeasure with me, the anonymous writer addressed the envelope to The Honorable Waggoner Carr—then scratched out "The Honorable":

La Grange, Texas

To Waggoner Carr:

You tore your pants with me - Big Boy.

Not respectfully,
A Voter

TOUGH LOVE

A Bell County man registered a legal complaint against a woman who, according to him, agreed to go on a date with him for $10, then changed her mind and kept his money. He filed charges with a Justice of the Peace for "theft by false pretext." Someone sent a copy of it to one of my assistants with this note written across the bottom of the form:

"Show this to Waggoner Carr. It looks like the kind of complaint that will need the combined assistance of all the State's prosecuting talent to get a conviction."

WHO ELSE ARE YOU HIDING?

The late Homer Garrison was the highly respected head of the Texas Department of Public Safety for a number of years, but the author of this letter held neither of us in very high esteem:

Richland Springs, Texas

Mr. Waggoner Carr
Austin, Texas

Sir:

Did you intend your letter of June 28 as an insult? We would not give a dime for your advice or opinion on any matter.

You know that I asked for information in regard to the accusations being made against us and our posterity by secret agents that are pretending to be working for the departments of the state.

Is it not a fact that Homer Garrison is in a military reserve by the federal government, and that he has been operating under your name?

Is it not a fact that when a girl reaches the age of sixteen, she is forced to sign an affidavit pledging allegiance to Homer Garrison or be deprived of her right to be a free woman?

A LANDSLIDE VICTORY TOO CLOSE TO CALL

Calling himself a "20th Century Future Times Prophet," a Liberty, Texas man sent this unsolicited notarized statement during my Senate race against Senator John Tower:

It is my sincere and most firm prediction that Senator John Tower, presently serving in the U.S. Senate, will be reelected by a large majority. I will vote for him, but I do not predict according to the way I vote. There may be a runoff.

★ ★ ★

EVEN IF WE WIN, WE LOSE

Beaumont, Texas

Atty. General
Austin, Texas

Dear Sir:

I have a complaint to make. Port Arthur has a bingo game on the air on channel 4-KPAC they say they get their rules from Austin. They call it a "cover all" bingo and when you bingo you have 2 phone numbers to call. One local and one long distance. Now here is my complaint.

Monday, Dec. 14th, my roomer Mr. covered his card. I rang the phone for 17 minutes. No one answered the phone, it rang and rang. Now if you make the rules why don't they have a system like they do on the March of Dimes, so we can see the operators and the Pot was $1,425 now thats a lot of money to lose. After the bingo channel 4 announced they had a winner. I rang the phone before they gave the last two numbers out. Anyway why can't we have a legitimate game like we used to. The churches helped our boys and girls to go to college helped the milk fund the crippled children. We women don't have any entertainment, but bingo and we have to go to Louisiana to play bingo and here we have to go out and beg for a card and then when we win, we can't get the call through. Please look into this and make them answer the phone and not make it look crooked.

THIS GUY WAS M-E-A-N!

Bowie County Jail
Boston, Texas

Dear Judge _____:

The strangest thing happened to me today. After I finished constructing the enclosed documents, I was reading the paper and came across a most interesting article. My Psychiatrist was committed to an Insane Asylum. Can you imagine that? All the time I thought he was all right and I was crazy, but its just the reverse. I'm just mean, not crazy.

Would you be so kind as to request Judge _____ that I wish to appeal my case on the records he has ordered up from the sentencing court here. They should be sufficient for an appeal and in the meantime I would like to be committed to the penitentiary awaiting the results so that I might get some medical attention and gain.

Should the Appeal court so desire, you could grant me a speedy review first and then order me committed. Whichever way is most suitable to the court.

I regret having caused so much trouble but I had a certain amount of bitterness that had to be expelled in some way and the authority was closest at hand.

I would write Trial Judge _____ instead of the Appeal Court but I'm going to have to kill him and District Attorney _____ when I get out.

Cordially,

THERE OUGHT TO BE A LAW!

El Paso, Texas

Please look at the enclosed folders, Mr. Carr, and you will see the drastic need for controlling the animal population and reducing breeding in the animal world.

When the next legislature convenes, please give your support to a law that would impose heavy penalties for allowing a female dog or cat to run at large while she is in season.

IT'S PAYBACK TIME

Nacogdoches, Texas

Attorney General Waggoner Carr

Sir I am writing you for manny time I have cast in votes for you and you have been successful to win Now I am asking you now will you help me I am running for Queen for the School PTA and the one rais the most

will be crown as Queen for the next So I am asking you
will you send me a donation by the 15 of Sept
Will thank you in advance.

FREAKS OF NATURE DEFINED

Concord, California

Dear Sir:

I am endeavoring to trace down a wild rumor. If you
can help me, I will be very grateful.

What is the law in your state regarding sexual relations
with animals, most particularly sheep? Do you have any
record of freak progeny being produced by such
relations between man and sheep?

My interest is purely academic. I am a student of
genetics and, though I find it impossible to believe,
have been told by an eye-witness that such freaks in
nature have occurred.

Thank you for any help which you might give.

The following was excerpted from the response
letter written by Assistant Attorney General Alan
Minter:

Dear Mr. _____:

Enclosed you will find Article 524, Vernon's Texas Penal
Code, "the law" in Texas concerning your topic request.
There is no record kept, that I know of, concerning
freak progeny produced by such relations.

Historically, cases in which beasts exercise an
aphrodisiacal influence over human beings have been
classified under "beast-fetishism, zoophilia erotica,
unnatural abuse or sodomy, and violations of animals or
bestiality." Most modern authorities follow the usual

terminology in describing bestiality and pederasty under the general term of sodomy.

In *Genesis* (Chap. XIX) there is the distinction between sodomy, i.e. cohabitation with a person of the same sex, and bestiality, i.e. cohabitation with an animal. Jurists use the terminology sodomy in terms of sex and in terms of genus.

Psychologically, the violation of animals if termed "bestiality" is when there may be no psychopathological condition but only low morality and/or sexual desire. Such may have been the case when Frederick the Great took the following action in a case of a cavalry man who had committed bestiality with a mare: "The fellow is a pig, and shall be reduced to the infantry." On the other hand, if termed "zooerasty," the condition may be of a pathological nature such as constitutional neuroses or a perverse condition acquired through fetishistic influences.

WE WANT WHAT'S BEST FOR YOU!

Troy, N.Y.

Dear Mr. Carr:

Just read a report that you are being shadowed by the FBI as you are suspected of having films of the progress of Jack Ruby being escorted thru the Dallas Police security lines by a highly placed member of the U. S. Justice Dep't.

As you may or may not know, your life is in danger and your safety, health and longevity lies in publicizing these photos, *NOT* in concealment or hiding them, and I do wish you long life and all the health that would normally be yours except for the situation that you are alleged to be in as per the news article.

Nowadays there are no more stories of the Texas

style spender in the papers or goodhearted jokes of the
Texan in the big city and the cause of all this is and can
be laid at the doorstep of Pedernales Causeway. We in
the North are not all dumb, what goes on in Texas was
not invented there...cows were in New York long
before Texas was thought of....$teer$ also.

So, don't be foolish and think you are safe as long as
you are hiding copies of that film if you are as stated by
the news account, your safety lies in making the other
guy RUN by seeing to it that these pictures are spread
around and on the SQUARE. Good luck and health and
long life.

THEY DID ME WRONG, JUDGE

A writ of habeas corpus may be filed to require a
person be brought before a judge or court for investigation of restraint of that person's liberty, as a
protection against illegal imprisonment. We processed
a number of such applications each year, but none
quite as novel as from this inmate, who admitted he
had burglarized a house of "guns, clothes, money and
a few small items," yet contended that his acts were
"constitutionally protected because he was in the
process of escaping from an illegal confinement."

Stating why his original imprisonment was "an
illegal confinement and therefore a criminal act," he
continued the application with the following:

"A person on escape must continually be running. He can not seek employment or sink roots in a community. To do so is to face the constant hazard of exposure and reconfinement.

"In olden times a horse, blanket and rifle were sufficient to enable an escapee to live in public domain. This is no longer possible. To run today, a person must have private means of movement along the nation's highways. This requires a car, something which cannot be trapped in a blind canyon. In the absence of funds, theft of such means is the only alternative.

"The possession of an auto is an empty thing without fuel. Fuel must be stolen or purchased. A tank of stolen fuel is no good for more than 300 miles, while a theft of a few dollars means several tanks of fuel plus food and shelter for a time.

"The right to escape would be an empty and meaningless thing if the exercise of that right were limited to the immediate environs of the locality of confinement. The right must, of necessity, be co-extensive with that of the United States and its territories since the right finds its roots in the 9th Amendment of the United States Constitution.

"In the instant case, petitioner escaped illegal confinement in Washington; working where and when he could, he made his way to Denver, Colorado. In a destitute condition he resorted to theft by bailee when he rented a car, and wrote a hot check to procure transportation, and to obtain funds to continue his flight. After which, Colorado joined the chase.

"Arrested in Oklahoma, he was returned to Colorado; making bond, he returned to Oklahoma. In Oklahoma once again he was arrested and, breaking jail at Sulphur, Oklahoma, he fled to New York. In New York he found employment.

"Shortly thereafter, he was unemployed and once more running. This time toward South America and a haven in Brazil, or on to another continent if possible. At the Texas border, he was apprehended a few miles from the relative haven of Mexico.

"Here again his rights guaranteed him by the Constitution of the United States and Texas was ignored.

"More sinned against than sinning, he was sentenced to serve a term of not less than two nor more than four years in prison. Every alleged act of crime he has done has been more than counterbalanced by the crime done to him in the name of society of which he is a part.

"The imprisonment from which he escaped was unlawful, and every act done to make good that escape is fully covered by allowable force including the crime to which he pleaded guilty, whether guilty or not."

SNAKES ALIVE!

While I was Attorney General, an inmate of the Texas prison system petitioned the U.S. Supreme Court from being subjected to cruel and unusual punishment and denied due process of law. The facts stated in the case were:

1. That the petitioner, since childhood, had an uncontrollable fear of snakes so extensive that even the sight of a snake caused him to "blackout" and flee without comprehension of any other physical danger to himself—off an embankment into the path of an automobile, etc.;

2. That he had been assigned to a prison farm unit infested with snakes;

3. That, while at the unit, he had been twice bitten by snakes, almost killed by a guard who thought he was trying to escape, developed an ulcer and became so frightened and mentally disturbed that he tried to kill himself; and,
4. That he was, at the time of the suit, hospitalized with the ulcer, but still assigned to a snake-infested prison unit.

The arguments stated in the case were:

1. That the petitioner sought redress in the Court of Criminal Appeals, on the basis that the assignment knowingly placed him in a position where he would daily come into contact with snakes, was cruel and unusual punishment, and made his imprisonment more onerous than the law permits;
2. That it denied him due process of law, endangering his life as well as mental and physical safety unduly; in that the guards of the prison would shoot to kill a running prisoner and the petitioner was endangered in that upon contact with a snake he became a fleeing prisoner totally blank of mind, and incapable of hearing, obeying or comprehending an order to halt;
3. That the court denied this application without hearing and without written order;
4. That denial of a petition for habeas corpus without a hearing, and without a written order, where facts are raised which are de ha the criminal record—is a denial of due process of law in violation of the 14th Amendment to the U.S. Constitution; and,

5. That his prison classification and assignment to such prison farm or field work in face of these facts, apparent on face of the records, was a cruel and unusual punishment such as is prohibited by the 8th Amendment to the U.S. Constitution.

The redress sought was:

"To be relieved of any farm or field assignments, or to other assignments, where he would be likely to come in contact with a snake."

☆ J. F. K. ☆

This book is generally light and humorous, but the stories in this chapter are more serious in nature. They represent a small portion of my personal experiences while officially involved in one of the most dramatic events of this century—the assassination of President John F. Kennedy.

THE FATAL TRIP

It was in November 1963 when President John F. Kennedy embarked on what he considered an important and politically necessary trip to Texas that ended prematurely with his tragic assassination in Dallas. As Texas Attorney General, I was one of the officials invited to greet the President upon his arrival in San Antonio, and to accompany the presidential party to Houston, Ft. Worth, Dallas, and Austin before he returned to the nation's capital.

Governor Connally was already in San Antonio when Ernestine and I joined Nellie Connally and a few others in a private flight from Austin to San Antonio's International Airport, where a huge crowd awaited the Chief Executive's arrival. When Air Force One landed and taxied to the reserved area, President and Mrs. Kennedy stepped out to the crowd's roar of approval and received an official welcome to Texas by the governor and a host of state, county, and city officials. I hadn't seen the President since the campaign rally in Lubbock three years earlier and it was good to shake his hand.

The San Antonio schedule included a parade through the city and then to Kelly Air Force Base for a reception and the President's initial Texas address. From there we returned to the airport where Ernestine and I joined Vice President and Mrs. Johnson in Air Force Two for departure for Houston.

Arriving in Houston, the Kennedys, Johnsons, and Connallys led the parade in special automobiles and the rest of the presidential party followed in cars and busses to the Rice Hotel, then departed for the coliseum. President Kennedy made another impressive speech there.

The matter of logistics is one of the most important aspects of a presidential tour. So many people are involved that a disruption in transportation can cause all sorts of problems—such as being left standing at the gate if you are not there when the President or Vice President is ready to leave.

After the Houston banquet, our bus arrived at the airport just as the pilot started the engines on Air Force Two. Air Force One was ready to depart and Vice President Johnson was giving his own crew orders to leave when we heard a woman's voice crying loudly from the back of the plane, "This plane is not about to leave until my husband gets here!" When Johnson asked what she said, someone explained that the Speaker of the House wasn't aboard yet and his wife was almost in hysterics for fear the plane might leave without him. The Vice President calmly instructed the crew to call on the radio and try to locate the Speaker. They relayed the message that he had missed the bus and was on the way in a police car with sirens wailing. Johnson called Air Force One and told the President that Air Force Two would be delayed slightly, but would catch up by the time they reached Ft. Worth. Air Force One was in a holding pattern when the Vice President's plane arrived and they landed right on time. The moral is this: Never underestimate the power of a distraught wife! This one held up two of the most influential men of the world's most powerful government until she once again had her husband by her side!

The next morning, we all attended a breakfast in the ballroom of the Texas Hotel in Ft. Worth. The President arrived on time, but the First Lady came in about thirty minutes later and charmed the whole crowd with her presence. After his speech, President Kennedy passed along the head table acknowledging the participants. When he stopped by my chair, we shook hands and he told me how pleased he and Mrs. Kennedy were with the great reception they had received thus far, and that they certainly felt welcome. He said he had been advised that I was leaving the entourage to keep a speaking engagement, but would rejoin them that evening for the State dinner. I thanked him for his concern and said I would look forward to seeing them in Austin.

The presidential party left the hotel and Ernestine and I headed in opposite directions. She returned to Austin to prepare for the final event that evening at

Austin's Palmer Auditorium and I went to the airport to board a private plane to Dumas, in the northern panhandle, for my speaking engagement.

About an hour later, a sniper killed President Kennedy in the Dallas parade. I was totally unaware of this awful turn of events until I arrived in Dumas. I couldn't believe it at first. We canceled the speech, of course, and watched the shocking news reports on television for a brief time before my plane was refueled and I returned to Austin to be available for whatever official duties might be necessary.

A PROPHETIC EVENT

Sometime after the fatal trip to Dallas, I learned about an unusual event which involved a close friend of mine during John F. Kennedy's earlier visit to San Antonio. He was attorney Bert Thompson, who served as my Bexar County manager in my statewide campaigns. His law office was located in a downtown high-rise building that overlooked a historic Catholic church President Kennedy wanted to see.

Bert knew the President would be there and, having this wonderful view of the church, he brought his binoculars to the office that morning for a closer look at the famous visitor. When the official party arrived at the church, Bert stood at his office window peering through the binoculars trained on every move the President made—until two Secret Service men suddenly rushed through his office door and grabbed him. Only by some fast talking was my friend able to

convince them he was merely an interested spectator
... not a potential sniper.

SPECIAL SECURITY

The situation was extremely tense immediately
following President Kennedy's assassination, with
speculation about a conspiracy to kill other government officials.

Governor Connally was seriously wounded during
the Dallas parade and recuperated in a two-room
hospital suite on the top floor of the Dallas hospital
after his surgery. I visited him there to brief him on the
progress of my investigation of the fateful event.

State troopers closely guarded the entire floor on a
24-hour vigil and stayed outside the door to his suite.
I waited in the outer room of the suite to see him when
I noticed the outside windows were covered with
sheets and a curved metal plate stood between these
sheets and the windows—to deflect any exterior gun-
fire that might come through.

My visit with him took 15 minutes or so, during
which he sat on the side of his bed with the aid of a
nurse while she inspected the condition of his wounds.
He seemed to be in considerable pain but listened
intently. At the end of my report he said, "Well, it
appears to me you have everything under control. I'm
confident that you're doing everything you can." At
that moment I thought, I only wish I had that much
confidence in myself!

TEMPORARY QUARTERS

While in the hospital, Governor Connally appointed four of us to represent Texas at President Kennedy's funeral. I joined Lt. Governor Preston Smith, Speaker of the House Byron Tunnell, and Chairman of the State Democratic Executive Committee Eugene Locke in this mission.

Upon our arrival in Washington, we visited briefly with the new President in the Executive Office Building adjacent to the White House. He was presiding from there, I learned, because the Kennedy staff was in no apparent hurry to move out of the White House to make room for him. During our thirty-minute visit, we talked about the horror and gravity of the situation and dire assessments of the turn of world events. He appeared to me to be still considerably affected by the shock of the assassination.

An autographed photo of this meeting hangs on my law office wall. It is interesting to note that there is a dot beneath the "B" in Lyndon B. Johnson's signature. I was told this dot indicates the signature was written personally by the President, rather than another person or a machine.

TEXANS WERE PERSONAE NON GRATA

The second order of business, after we landed in Washington to attend the Kennedy funeral, was to find a place to rent the pinstripe trousers, long tail coats, and tall black hats we were to wear.

Late that evening, having accomplished the dress requirement, we were having a snack in the hotel dining room. Someone at our table said something unintentionally funny and we all laughed spontaneously. Suddenly, a man sitting at a table nearby jumped up from his seat, loudly berated us for laughing at a time of such national sorrow, and told us we should be ashamed of ourselves for such conduct.

We apologized and tried to explain, but when he found out we were from Texas, we got it with both barrels. He called us every dirty name he could think of and blamed Texas for the President's assassination. Realizing there was no point in arguing with him and noting that others in the room were glaring at us, we quickly departed. Washington at that time was no place to be if you were a Texan!

THE WASHINGTON PRESS CORPS

Before going to the cathedral for the funeral, I talked with a White House staff member and explained that Texas laws authorized a Court of Inquiry —which I could convene as the Attorney General—to establish the facts surrounding the assassination through a public hearing.

After talking with the President and getting his approval, the staff member instructed me to call a press conference for members of the Texas press corps in Washington, and say only that I would hold a Court of Inquiry on the assassination as soon as I returned to Texas. He emphasized that I should limit my remarks to those simple facts and not reveal, under any circumstances, that I had discussed this with the White House or had White House approval. I agreed and called to make arrangements for what I thought would be a very short speech to a small group of Texas reporters.

When this conversation ended, it was time to attend the funeral and our delegation walked to the cathedral and took our seats near the main entrance. This provided a good vantage point to observe the array of world leaders and dignitaries in attendance. I particularly remember France's President Charles DeGaulle, whose height was such that he towered over everyone near him as he left the cathedral. After the funeral, the President's casket was placed on a horse-drawn carriage and the somber procession started its long walk to Arlington National Cemetery for the burial.

Instead of joining the procession, I returned to my hotel room to get ready for the press conference. The procession took much longer than I anticipated, but I didn't think it proper to hold the conference until it was over. I remained in my room watching it on television. It was at least an hour after the press conference was supposed to start, when the last rites ended.

The expression on my face must have mirrored my shock and disbelief at what I saw when I entered the conference room. The large crowd of reporters, representative from all major networks and the foreign press, microphones on the podium, TV cameras, etc., were a far cry from the intimate little gathering I expected. Somehow the word leaked out, as it usually does in Washington, and I stood facing what looked to me like the entire media world.

On my way to the podium someone sarcastically yelled, "Are you really the Attorney General of Texas?" I ignored the remark and took the podium to read my prepared statement, worded something like this: "Ladies and Gentlemen, my name is Waggoner Carr and I am the Attorney General of the State of Texas. I came here to attend President Kennedy's funeral and am leaving for Texas this evening. Tomorrow, I will call a Court of Inquiry for the purpose of investigating the facts surrounding the assassination of President Kennedy in our state. I am now departing for the airport and will not answer questions at this time."

Having waited so long for my arrival and then hearing that brief statement with no opportunity to question me did not help my popularity. Several people shouted questions and insults when I left the podium. I kept my commitment to the White House, although I had difficulty stifling the urge to tell those impolite so-and-so's what I thought about their behavior. They followed me out of the room, shouting at me all the way into the lobby. If that wasn't bad enough, I compounded it with a wrong decision.

One of the national TV cameramen ran up to me and said that his network was delayed in picking up my statement and asked if I'd please return to the podium and do it over so his network could air it along with the others. Right then I missed a golden opportunity to keep my mouth shut. I should have kept walking, but I foolishly complied and by the time I made my way back through the "pack of howling wolves" again, I heard more insults and expletives than I care to recall. Only by entering an elevator just as the door started to close was I able to avoid them and return to my hotel room to pack.

My plane ride home that evening wasn't very enjoyable.

PRESIDENTIAL SUPPORT

Returning to Texas, I found considerable hostility to my plan for a Court of Inquiry from political detractors and certain members of the press. They said I was using the assassination to gain publicity for personal and political benefit. The only way to get it in proper perspective was for the White House to acknowledge full support.

I informed the President about this problem and, within a few days, White House Assistant Barefoot Sanders and Herbert Miller of the Justice Department appeared with me at a press conference in the Attorney General's office in Austin. That gave me the credibility I needed.

The Texas law required the judge of a Court of Inquiry be a Justice of the Peace. Acutely aware of the world-wide implications, as well as the stress and tension of such a hearing, I was concerned that the selection process might take some time because we needed to appoint the most capable person available.

I had already appointed two outstanding Texas attorneys as special counsel to assist me in the Court of Inquiry—Robert Storey, retired dean of the Southern Methodist University Law School and Leon Jaworski, former president of the Texas State Bar Association.

By this time, however, both the FBI and CIA had started their own investigations and Congress appointed its own special investigating committee. The situation developed into a three-ring circus atmosphere, with competition between these four entities that bordered on the ridiculous. It was then that President Johnson appointed a special commission empowered to investigate the assassination and this eventually ended the unnecessary bickering and duplicity of effort. The media immediately dubbed it the Warren Commission.

Headed by Supreme Court Chief Justice Earl Warren, the Commission included these prominent Americans:

Sen. Richard Russell (D-Ga.), Chairman, Senate Armed Services Committee;

Sen. John Sherman Cooper (R-Ken.), former U.S. Ambassador to India;

Rep. Hale Boggs (D-La.), House Majority Whip;

Rep. Gerald R. Ford (R-Mich.), later U.S. President;

Allen W. Dulles, former director, Central Intelligence Agency;

John J. McCloy, former president of International Bank for Reconstruction and Development, former U.S. High Commissioner for Germany, and former Assistant Secretary of War during WW II.

TWO-DAY STANDOFF

Shortly after President Johnson appointed the Warren Commission, he requested that I combine the upcoming investigation by the Texas Court of Inquiry with the Commission's investigation. Since the state and federal government needed each other's resources for this effort, I agreed. The President suggested that I visit with Chief Justice Earl Warren as soon as possible to work out a cooperative effort. Mr. Jaworski accompanied me to Washington, D.C., for this purpose.

Attorney General Robert Kennedy was still in mourning at that time and, in his absence, the White House had arranged for Assistant Attorney General Nicholas Katzenbach to set up the meeting with the Chief Justice. To my complete surprise, Mr. Katzenbach reported to us that the Chief Justice refused to see us until we agreed that Texas would drop any plans for an investigation and any thought of participating in the Warren Commission investigation!

Word had come to me earlier that Earl Warren, while viewing the Kennedy casket in the Capitol rotunda, had said Texas was to blame for the assassination. I was determined not to turn our investigation over to a man who had already "convicted" my state. I told Mr. Katzenbach that under no circumstances would I, as Attorney General of Texas, agree to Warren's demand but that, in an effort to be cooperative as the President had suggested, Mr. Jaworski and I were willing to try to work something out if he would see us.

It developed into a Warren-Carr two-day standoff, with Katzenbach acting as go-between. Late in the afternoon of the second day, we sat in the Attorney General's office awaiting Katzenbach's return from another visit with Warren. When he came back, he told us that Warren remained adamant not to see us until we complied with his terms.

Completely frustrated and with little patience remaining, I advised Mr. Katzenbach that we were leaving for Texas on the next plane and when we arrived there I would convene the Court of Inquiry. I added that this would be a public hearing, as opposed to Warren's closed-door investigations, and we would let the world determine which one it liked best. We immediately departed for our hotel to check out, but by the time I reached my room, Mr. Katzenbach called to say the Chief Justice had agreed to meet with us that evening in his office in the Supreme Court building.

We had a frank discussion, courteous but firm. I told the Chief Justice that Texas would forego its immediate plans for a Court of Inquiry and participate in a joint investigation that would coordinate the investigative forces of both governments, with the following understanding:

1. That Texas would be an active participant in the investigation and that we would be given notice of all scheduled witness interviews and have the right to participate in the questioning of such witnesses;

2. That the Texas Attorney General would be responsible to see that all state and local agencies would forward to the Commission all evidence, documents, etc., pertinent to the investigation;

3. That when the investigation was completed, if we felt
   a. It had been fair to Texas,
   b. It had been thorough, and
   c. No evidence was withheld from the public, then I would report this to Governor Connally and the people of Texas and publicly agree with the Commission's conclusions;

4. That, on the other hand, if we felt that any of the requirements in a, b, or c had not been met, I would have the right to immediately convene a Texas Court of Inquiry to complete the investigation.

After considerable discussion, the Chief Justice agreed.

Early in the hearings, however, some witnesses were interrogated without notice to me so that I or my special counsel could be present. I promptly wrote to Chief Justice Warren reciting this violation to our agreement and stated that I was prepared to convene the Court of Inquiry.

I duly received notice of the next witness hearing, but it fell on a day when I could not be present, so Mr. Jaworski attended for me. He reported when he returned that the Chief Justice was quite upset over my "upstart" letter and felt it was not proper for the Attorney General of Texas to write such a letter to the Chief Justice of the Supreme Court. Jaworski also reported that Warren reinforced his dissatisfaction with me by requiring my representative to remove himself from the counsel table and sit in a straight chair in the corner of the room where he took notes while balancing a pad on his knees.

Notices were timely from then on and our working relationship gradually improved. Upon completion of the 10-month investigation, the Commission included this statement in its report to the President and the American people:

"In addition to the assistance afforded by federal agencies, the Commission throughout its inquiry had the cooperation of representatives of the city of Dallas and the State of Texas. The Attorney General of Texas, Waggoner Carr, aided by two distinguished lawyers of that state, Robert G. Storey of Dallas, retired dean of the Southern Methodist University Law School and former president of the American Bar Association, and Leon Jaworski, former president of the Texas State Bar Association, has been fully informed at all times as to the progress of the investigation, and has advanced such suggestions as he and his special assistants considered helpful to the accomplishments of the Commission's assignment. Attorney General Carr has promptly supplied the Commission with pertinent information possessed by Texas officials."

In a written report to Governor Connally, I stated my satisfaction with the Commission's work and agreed with its conclusions. My office forwarded a copy of this report to every state college library in Texas.

A SPECIAL NUMBER

Prior to the initial meeting of the Warren Commission, I took Dallas District Attorney Henry Wade and his assistant, Bill Alexander, to Washington for a meeting with Chief Justice Earl Warren.

We made hotel reservations for three single rooms but when we checked in, they had booked us into a suite with three bedrooms and a common living room instead. Caught up in the aura of intrigue that pervaded our mission, each of us was immediately suspicious about this unexpected arrangement, although we had no evidence then, or later, that this was so. Nevertheless, we thought it possible that the room could be bugged to record our conversations.

One of the items of information we brought with us was a copied portion of Lee Oswald's diary, including a particular Washington telephone number we planned to identify during the trip. Charged with the energies of the moment, we decided to call this number then and there and put on some kind of "show" for the benefit of potential eavesdroppers who might be listening in, if there were any.

We dialed the number and it rang, but we hung up immediately without saying a word when a heavily accented voice at the other end answered, "Russian Embassy!"

GETTING TO KNOW THE CHIEF JUSTICE

Among other problems facing the country at the time of the Kennedy assassination was the upheaval of civil rights issues that began in the 1950s. The Chief Justice himself was the verbal target of the ultra conservative faction across the nation, who clamored for his removal from office because of the Supreme Court's liberal decisions on civil rights.

Assistant District Attorney Bill Alexander probably knew more about the facts surrounding the assassination than any other living person at that time. Our trip to meet with Chief Justice Warren was Bill's first time in the nation's capital. He seemed awed by the setting and justifiably impressed with his own place in history at the time.

Sitting at the table where he could see the Supreme Court building and the Capitol dome through the windows behind the Chief Justice of the Supreme Court was a humbling experience. Bill quickly overcame it, however, when Warren asked him about Jack Ruby's actions the night following the assassination. Alexander responded with all of the importance he could muster in words to this effect:

"Well, Mr. Chief Justice, my investigation has shown that on the night following the assassination,

Ruby went to his apartment in Oak Cliff, a suburb of Dallas, in a very nervous and emotional state. He didn't stay there long, but got in his car and headed toward town and to his strip joint called 'The Carousel.' On the way to The Carousel he observed a billboard along the street. He stopped his car, got out and went over to that billboard, returned to his car to get a camera, then took a picture of the billboard before getting back into his car and drove away."

The Chief Justice said, "Mr. Alexander, I will not interrupt you often, but it is important that I understand the significance of each detail you tell me. What was on that billboard Mr. Ruby was so interested in?"

Bill seemed to slump down in his chair, as if he would rather not have to answer the question, but replied, "Well, Mr. Chief Justice, it read 'IMPEACH EARL WARREN'."

The silence was deafening for a long moment until Bill, in his best courtroom manner added, "Mr. Chief Justice, it wasn't anything but a little bitty old sign. It didn't amount to nothing."

That broke the tension. The Chief Justice smiled and said, "Well, Mr. Alexander, let me say this, sir. That particular sign always looks bigger to me than it does to anyone else!"

NOTHING IS FREE

Prior to attending one of the early meetings of the Warren Commission, Leon Jaworski and I stopped by the White House for a brief conference with President Johnson.

The President said he would appreciate our coming back afterwards and reporting on the progress made before we returned to Texas. I told him we were scheduled on the last commercial flight available that day because I had to be in the Attorney General's office the following morning. The President assured us that he would arrange necessary air transportation if we missed the commercial flight.

When we arrived back at the White House later in the evening, he was in the pool enjoying a swim with Mrs. Johnson, Congressman Homer Thornberry, and a couple of other people whose names I don't recall. We conferred with the President at the pool's edge for quite some time and when we concluded the briefing, our commercial flight had already departed.

President Johnson asked White House Assistant Jack Valenti to arrange for transportation. A White House car delivered us to a sleek little nine-passenger presidential jet at nearby Andrews Air Force Base. The flight crew stood at attention when we drove up alongside. The ground crew quickly put our bags aboard and we taxied for take-off.

The Marine Corps steward, wearing a starched white jacket, came forward after we reached cruising altitude to ask if we would like a drink before our meal. He mixed them in the galley, served us, and we sipped them leisurely while discussing various events of the day. Meanwhile, he prepared a table and served a hot meal we thoroughly enjoyed.

Just before I got off the plane at Austin, the steward stood at attention and announced, "Gentlemen, it has been a pleasure to have you aboard this craft. Any friend of the President is a friend of ours and we hope we have the pleasure of serving you again." We both thanked him for the excellent food and thoughtful service. Then he said, "Now, gentlemen, that will be $1.67 each for your drink and meal." (Remember, this was in 1963!)

I couldn't resist telling Leon, "We've had a nonstop 1,500 mile jet trip with a pilot, co-pilot, navigator, and flight steward . . . a great drink . . . and a delightful meal . . . all for $1.67. That ain't bad!" We learned later there was strict accounting for food service to civilians on government aircraft.

EVEN PUBLIC PHONES WERE SUSPECT

During one of my early trips to Washington for the Warren Commission investigations, I stopped by the office of Attorney General Robert Kennedy to person-ally inform him about the efforts of the State of Texas to determine facts surrounding the assassination of his brother.

Concluding this friendly visit, I asked one of his assistants for direction to a telephone where I could call several Texas Congressmen who were personal friends of mine. He directed be to a pay phone in the hall where I could have private conversations. He was courteous in warning me not to use one certain pay phone adjacent to the office, inasmuch as it was bugged!

THE INFAMOUS BOOK DEPOSITORY

Several Warren Commission members visited the assassination site in Dallas during the latter days of their investigation and I went there to assist them. We talked with Lee Harvey Oswald's book depository co-workers who told us about his actions on the day of the assassination.

We had Oswald's rifle and each of us sat exactly where he did when he fired it, in front of the sixth story depository window where the three spent cartridges were found. Each, in turn, rested the unloaded gun against the book cartons as he had done to steady it, took aim at an imaginary limousine target, pulled the trigger, and activated the bolt. Our interest in doing this was to determine if it was reasonable that Oswald could have fired it three times in the time span of five and one-half seconds. This fact was necessary to decide if someone else also might have been firing at the same time.

The Italian manufactured rifle seemed clumsy to me and I couldn't operate it fast enough, but Commission member John McCloy had no difficulty performing the feat. He had a military background and was convinced that anyone with any military rifle experience could do it. With one shell already in the chamber, it only required two bolt actions.

Oswald not only had military rifle experience as a former Marine sharpshooter, but the investigation revealed that he had practiced firing this particular rifle at a local firing range.

The FBI proved conclusively that Oswald could and did fire the weapon that fast.

PRIOR INTENT TO KILL

Major General Edwin A. Walker, Jr., became a politically active and controversial figure following his resignation from the Army in the early 1960s and his name made frequent newspaper headlines and TV news features.

At 9 p.m. on April 10, 1963, Walker was sitting at his desk in his Dallas home, when an outside shot rang out. He narrowly escaped death from a rifle bullet that passed just above his head. The shooting remained unsolved for nine months until the Warren Commission investigation.

Lee Harvey Oswald's widow, Marina — in her testimony before the Warren Commission in February 1964 — stated under oath that when Oswald returned home on the night of the Walker shooting, he told her he had been planning the attempt for two months. She testified:

"When he came back (to their apartment) I asked him what happened. He was very pale. I don't remember the exact time, but it was very late and he told me not to ask him any questions. He told me only that he had shot at General Walker. When he learned on the radio and in the newspapers the next day that he had missed, he said that he 'was very sorry that he had not hit him.'"

Three days later Oswald showed his wife a notebook containing photographs of General Walker's home and a map of the area where it was located.

In January 1964 Marina Oswald and her business manager, James Martin, told her brother-in-law Robert Oswald that Lee had once threatened to shoot Vice President Richard M. Nixon. When Marina

Oswald testified before the Commission on June 11, 1964, she stated that a few days before her husband's departure from Dallas to New Orleans on April 24, 1963, "he finished reading a morning newspaper and put on a good suit. I saw that he took a pistol. I asked him where he was going and why he was getting dressed. He answered, 'Nixon is coming. I want to go and have a look.'" He also said that he would use the pistol if the opportunity arose. She reminded him that after the Walker shooting he had promised her never to repeat such an act. Marina related the events which followed. "I called him into the bathroom and I closed the door and I wanted to prevent him and then I started to cry. And I told him that he shouldn't do this, and that he had promised me. I remember that I held him. We actually struggled for several minutes and then he quieted down."

The Commission concluded that Marina Oswald might have misunderstood her husband. Nixon was not in Dallas at that time. However, on April 23, 1963, Vice President Lyndon Johnson was in Dallas on a visit which had been publicized in the Dallas newspapers throughout April.

THE RUBY MYSTERY

Jack Ruby's bizarre shooting of Lee Harvey Oswald before a nationwide television audience is still difficult to believe. The event has lent itself to many rumors and speculations that persist to this day. What was determined about Ruby's shooting of Oswald and how did it happen?

In Dallas, after a person was charged with a felony, the County Sheriff ordinarily took custody of and assumed responsibility for that prisoner's safekeeping. In cases of unusual importance, the Dallas City Police sometimes transported prisoners to the county jail.

Officials thus decided to move Oswald from the city jail, where he was taken after his arrest by the Dallas police, to the county jail on Sunday morning. They planned to have an armored truck leave the basement of the city jail as a decoy, followed by a car containing only security officers. A police car transporting Oswald would follow. A lead car was to precede the entire convoy.

Under heavy escort, Oswald had moved about ten feet from the door of the basement toward his designated car when some 40 to 50 newsmen surged forward, poking microphones at him, taking flash photos over and around him, and shouting questions in his face. With all eyes on Oswald, Jack Ruby passed between a newsman and a detective at the edge of the straining crowd. Holding a .38 caliber revolver with his right hand extended, Ruby stepped forward quickly and fired a single bullet into Oswald's abdomen before the startled lawmen could grab him.

How did Ruby get there and why?

One of Jack Ruby's employees at The Carousel had called him earlier that day, asking him to send her some money. With the money and his pistol, which he always had with him when he carried much cash, he drove to the Western Union office near the city jail. He observed a large crowd of onlookers near the jail.

The Commission established with precision the time of certain events leading up to the shooting. Minutes before Oswald appeared in the basement, Ruby was in the Western Union office located in the same block on Main Street, some 350 feet from the top of the Main Street ramp to the jail. The time stamped on the money order which he sent and the receipt found in his pocket established that the order was accepted for transmission at 11:17 a.m. Ruby was then observed departing the office and walking in the direction of the police building one block away. As he approached the Main Street ramp, the lead car driven by Lt. Pierce emerged from the basement onto Main Street and momentarily diverted the attention of the officer guarding the ramp entrance. Ruby walked down the open ramp into the basement to see what was going on and stood behind the front rank of newsmen and police officers crowded together awaiting the transfer of Oswald to the county jail. No more than 30 seconds later, as Oswald exited from the basement door at 11:21 a.m., Ruby moved quickly and, without speaking, fired that fatal shot.

During its ten-month investigation, the Warren Commission made extensive inquiry into the backgrounds and relationships of both Oswald and Ruby to determine if they knew each other or were involved in a plot of any kind with each other or other persons. It was unable to find any credible evidence to support the rumors linking Oswald and Ruby directly or indirectly. All assertions that Oswald was seen in the company of Ruby at The Carousel were thoroughly investigated, but could not be confirmed.

RETROSPECTION

At this writing in 1992—almost 29 years since President Kennedy was assassinated—controversy still rages over whether Lee Harvey Oswald acted alone or was part of a conspiracy.

Following the release of Oliver Stone's movie *JFK*, a story which Stone himself admits was riddled with fiction to make it more believable to the public, there has been media pressure for the government to make public its files of the Warren Commission.

Having been closely associated with many aspects of the actual situation, some of which are revealed in capsule form in this chapter, I strongly defend the efforts of the Warren Commission. Its comprehensive 16-volume written report to the President compelled the conclusion that Lee Harvey Oswald was the assassin of President Kennedy.

To emphasize the thoroughness of this report, the reader should know that immediately after the assassination, the FBI assigned some 80 additional agents to the Dallas office to assist in the investigation. The FBI conducted approximately 25,000 interviews of persons having possible relevant information and submitted over 2,300 reports totaling 25,400 pages to the Commission. The Secret Service conducted approximately 1,550 interviews and submitted 800 reports totaling some 4,600 pages. In addition to this information, the Commission took the testimony of 552 witnesses.

There was no credible evidence that Oswald was a conspirator. There was no evidence that the Soviet Union or Cuba was involved, nor did the Commission's investigation of Jack Ruby produce any grounds for believing that Ruby's killing of Oswald was part of a conspiracy. The same conclusions of no evidence of conspiracy was also reached independently by Attorney General Robert F. Kennedy; Secretary of State Dean Rusk; Secretary of Defense Robert McNamara; FBI Director J. Edgar Hoover; and others. Members of the Warren Commission were of such quality as to make ridiculous any suggestion that the Commission or any other element of our government, including President Johnson, conspired to assassinate President Kennedy.

I consider it ethically and morally wrong to produce a movie, TV production, book, etc., for great profit, that purposely misleads and causes distrust of our American government among our younger generations—who have no first-hand knowledge of the actual events nor have taken the opportunity to learn the facts.

Many Americans are paranoid conspiracy buffs. Some are still arguing over who shot President Lincoln. For them, there may never be enough facts to dispel their beliefs.

Lee Harvey Oswald must be smiling in his grave. He promised his wife Marina Oswald that someday he would be a very BIG man.

☆ L. B. J. ☆

SURPRISE CANDIDATE

When I was in the Texas Legislature, fellow member Dudley Dougherty ran for U.S. Senator against Lyndon B. Johnson. Johnson was well organized statewide with a large following and plenty of campaign funds. Dudley, on the other hand, was not well known, had little campaign funds other than his own personal money, and was not state-wide politically astute in the first place.

He telephoned me at my Lubbock office once during the campaign and said he was staying at the Hilton Hotel across the street and wondered if I could come over and talk with him. I had no advance knowledge that he even planned to be in town, so I was surprised. He knew I was supporting Johnson, but I said I'd come over. As a fellow legislator and a friend, it seemed the proper thing to do.

My second surprise was that all the drapes were drawn and he was completely alone. I asked if I could assist him in any way, such as arranging an interview with the editor of the Lubbock *Avalanche-Journal* or other members of the local news media.

His surprised me a third time when he refused that and said, "Under no circumstances do I want anyone to know I am in town. This is the first time during the campaign I have been able to go anywhere without Johnson or his campaign people knowing where I am."

Dougherty left Lubbock later that day, apparently a total success in not letting anyone there know that he was in pursuit of the United States Senate seat. He lost the election by a large majority, but that didn't surprise me at all!

LEST WE FORGET

Lyndon Johnson told me early in my political career that as long as I was in politics, there were two things I should always remember:
1. Never pass up a free meal; and
2. Never pass up an opportunity to go to the men's room!

JUST DON'T LET ME TRIP!

It is a rare privilege to receive a formal invitation to a White House social function and I was delighted when Ernestine and I were invited to a dinner there honoring the Justices of the United States Supreme Court.

Another Austin couple, University of Texas law professor Jerre Williams and his wife, Mary Pearl, also attended.

The dinner and speeches were excellent and at their conclusion, we moved to the White House rotunda area where a small military dance band played for after-dinner dancing. I noted that the President danced with one lady for a short time, then another and another, thoughtful to see that no lady returned home without being able to say she had danced with the President.

When he ended his dance with Mary Pearl, I cut in on her next partner. "Tell me, Mary Pearl," I asked, "what were you thinking while you danced with the President of the United States?"

Without missing a beat she said, "I was thinking 'keep moving feet, keep moving.'"

NOW THAT'S FREEDOM!

On several occasions, I rode with President Johnson as he drove around the LBJ Ranch in his Continental automobile or his Jeep. He enjoyed looking at his cattle, pointing out deer, watching them run, and staying in touch with the progress of his ranch employees. He used his shortwave radio to talk with his staff and others when ideas occurred to him.

One time he complained about his loss of freedom since becoming president, telling me this story as an example.

"You know, Waggoner," he began, "ever since I was a young boy, the very last thing I did every night before going to bed was go outside and relieve myself while looking up at the moon and millions of stars. As I stood there beholding that wondrous sight in complete privacy, I understood the true meaning of freedom. The first time I tried doing that out here after I became president, a Secret Service car spotlight was on me immediately and you know how painful it is to try to stop the flow once you're started."

He added, "They know better than that here now, but I don't have the freedom to do that at the White House, and I miss it."

TURN OUT THE LIGHTS
THE PARTY'S OVER

One of my trips to the nation's capital was to argue on behalf of Texas in two lawsuits before the Supreme Court. This was during my campaign for the U.S. Senate, and when I checked into the hotel, the desk clerk handed me a message from the White House.

I called the number and it was answered by the President himself, wanting to know if I was too tired to join the family for dinner and a brief visit with him. I said I'd already eaten on the flight but would be pleased to come for dessert. He sent a staff car to pick me up 15 minutes later.

Arriving there, I was escorted to the family quarters on the second floor where the President, Mrs. Johnson, Lynda Bird, a girlfriend of Lynda's, and Presidential Assistant Jake Jacobsen were seated at the dining room table. President Johnson talked on the telephone throughout the meal, prompting Mrs.

Johnson to comment that it looked like the President could take time off to eat and get off those telephone calls. I accepted a cup of coffee and dessert and engaged in small talk with the others.

He was scheduled to leave on a trip to the Far East the following day and the flurry of calls seemed necessary prior to his departure. It was almost 11 p.m. before he hung up the phone and finished his dinner — the ladies having already excused themselves and left. During the meal, aides brought important messages while Congressmen and other officials made brief appearances. I said I'd wait in the anteroom while he received them and he said fine, he'd be there shortly and we could chat. I thumbed through a number of magazines while he attended to that business. About midnight, he came in and started to sit down, but due to the late hour, I asked if he'd prefer to prepare for bed and I could talk to him while he was resting. I sat in the rocker next to his bed while he received a Senator who was running for reelection, then read and signed various papers.

At long last, he got in bed and we discussed several items of interest, primarily the Senate campaign and the latest Texas political news. Concerned that I was taking up too much of his precious time, I hinted several times that perhaps I should leave, but he kept saying no, he wanted to talk some more. Knowing he needed his rest and that I had an arduous day ahead myself, I finally took my leave around 1:30 a.m. We shook hands, he thanked me for coming and said we'd talk again when he returned from the East. As I closed his bedroom door, he called out, "Waggoner, will you turn off all the lights when you leave?"

Jake Jacobsen was waiting in the hall for me and after he said good night to the President we cut off the hall lights, but it was so dark we couldn't find the elevator. He switched the light on long enough for me to locate the elevator door and hold it open to light his way, then cut it off again.

I told Jake, "I've heard that the President turns out all the lights in the White House at night, but I thought it was just some writer's invention until now."

NO "CALL WAITING" HERE

Jake Jacobsen became my contact in the White House. To talk with him, I dialed an Austin unlisted number that was a direct line to the LBJ Ranch and a staff member connected me with the White House. I had the President's blessing during my Senate race to use this method to communicate with U.S. Senators and Representatives and others who might be helpful in the campaign.

One Sunday, I needed to talk with an East Texas Congressman in Washington. The ranch operator connected me with the White House operator who located the Congressman at his home. When he realized it was only me, he said with some disbelief, "I don't know how you managed this, but I must say you sure got my attention!"

UNWANTED GUEST

Each time I was in the White House, I was impressed by the endless interruptions President Johnson endured every waking hour. It gave me concern that each minute of my conversation might take valuable time away from his more important duties. On one such visit to the Oval Office, he asked me to sit on the couch and pulled his rocker close so we could talk.

The telephone rang in the middle of our discussion and he answered it from an extension set concealed in a nearby end table. While he talked, I glanced about the room to look at the interesting wall hangings and noticed a large horse fly winging its way toward the plate glass window. Its collision with the glass made an audible racket that was amplified further by constant buzzing up and down the window in search of a way to escape.

When he finished his telephone conversation, the President got up, grabbed a newspaper, rolled it up and made several swats at the droning insect while continuing our conversation. With a triumphant whack, he mortally wounded the intruder and returned to the rocker saying, "I don't know how these damned flies get in here!"

JEEP RIDE DIPLOMACY

Lyndon B. Johnson was a great storyteller, had a quick wit and, like Abraham Lincoln, could recall many humorous incidents to emphasize a point. Visitors to the LBJ Library in Austin or the LBJ

National Park at Stonewall can listen to recordings of the President telling some of these funny stories.

His serious side overshadowed much of his humor during the latter days of his presidency because of the Vietnam War. The gravity of some of these presidential decisions was brought home to me during a visit to the LBJ Ranch.

The President was driving White House Assistant Bill Moyers and me around the ranch in his Jeep. I was then a candidate for the U.S. Senate and mentioned that my opponent, incumbent John Tower, had criticized the conduct of the war and advocated discontinuing a presidential order that American pilots turn around just before they reached the border of Red China. It was a very controversial order because the Communists were using an area safe from U.S. raids to store munitions and supplies for attacks against our forces. The President also had ordered American pilots not to bomb Haiphong Harbor.

I told President Johnson I was somewhat sympathetic to the views expressed by Senator Tower and that I would appreciate anything he might tell me about the policies and how I might respond to Tower's criticism. He said he was aware of the controversy and that I should feel free to criticize them if I wanted to and do whatever necessary to win the election, which he wanted very much. Then he told me in general terms about the problems.

He described the situation of young American jet pilots flying at great speeds in weather that normally didn't allow them to see the ground. He ordered them not to cross the border of Red China, but to turn around at least 15 seconds before to avoid bombing or clashing with Red China forces. He said that if he, as

President, allowed this then Red China's leader could do the same.

"If I'm right about this, and I believe I am," he continued, "I could be starting WW III and killing our soldiers by the thousands instead of tens or hundreds."

He said Haiphong Harbor was open to all nations and that, while we were sitting there discussing this, ships were in that harbor from England, France, Russia, China, and other countries of the world. Then he added, "Waggoner, I could change this policy simply by picking up this Jeep's radio handset and ordering the harbor and the boundaries of China be bombed. It's just that easy. But if I do, then I run the risk of starting World War Three."

He concluded by saying if I felt he was wrong, I should say so in the campaign, but that was his reason for the policies. Realizing the terrible burden of his responsibilities, I could only say, "Mr. President, I know you are doing the best you can and I'm not going to criticize your decisions. I'm just glad you have to make those decisions, and not I!"

★ PEOPLE, PLACES ★
AND THINGS

WHAT WAS THAT NAME AGAIN?

Jim Underwood served as a public relations man during one of my statewide campaigns. He was well known in the Dallas area because of his work in radio broadcasting and we became constant companions during the campaign. He related this incident during one of our many flights:

A local area high school football team had reached the finals for the state championship and Jim Underwood was to call the play action broadcast on game day. Well in advance of the date, Jim got a players' roster to familiarize himself with names, numbers, and positions, to minimize the chance for mistakes during the broadcast. He noticed that the star player's last name was "Fulk" and it concerned him that he might mispronounce it during the excitement of the game and be accused of using an obscenity —which was cause for cutting a broadcast off the air in those days.

Underwood repeated the name "Jim Fulk, Jim Fulk, Jim Fulk," to himself over and over again every day until he felt comfortable that he could say it naturally, without making that "fatal mistake" during the broadcast.

Came the day of the big game and Jim opened the broadcast by introducing the name of each player to his radio audience. He saved Jim Fulk until last so he could concentrate on pronouncing it correctly. Finally, with great gusto he said, "Ladies and gentlemen, it is my genuine pleasure to introduce the star of the _____ High School team. Some think he is the greatest football player in the school's history and perhaps the entire state. I present to you now, Quarter-back Jim Fulk . . . spelled F-U-C-K!"

Immediately realizing what he had just said, Underwood was so devastated that he couldn't continue. He turned the microphone over to his assistant to call the remainder of the game.

LET'S ALL GET BEHIND HIM

Governor John Connally attended many public functions while he was in office and heard a variety of introductions. He heard none quite so confusing as this one, however, given before a large state-wide gathering in Austin, where he and wife Nellie were the guests of honor:

"I am indeed proud to present to you this distinguished man and his distinguished lady. It is said that behind every good man is a good woman, and in this case it is so fortunate that this good woman is behind this good man, because if this good woman was not behind this good man, there's no telling who this good man would be behind."

AUTHOR, AUTHOR

John Connally had a lot of class and was highly respected by friends and foes. Texas suffered a severe recession in the 1980s that seriously affected many people, including John and his business partners. He filed Chapter 11 bankruptcy action and publicly sold many cherished possessions to apply the proceeds against the debts.

During this stressful time, we appeared together in Houston to help raise money at a Bob Hope charity "roast." The crowd applauded and rose to its feet in unison to show their great respect when Connally approached the podium to deliver his roast lines. In his gracious way, he expressed his appreciation by saying:

"Ladies and gentlemen, Nellie and I deeply appreciate your welcome and it is great to be here with you good friends. As you know, we are having some financial difficulties at this time. We know you would like to help us and I have a way you can do that. You see, I am writing a book that you will find very interesting and each of you can buy a copy. It will be published soon." He paused and added with a grin, "I'm already into Chapter 11."

MEMORY LOSS

Bob Hope has held a number of charity benefits in Port Arthur, Texas, for the Hughen School for Crippled Children and Adults. I participated in four of these, including the 1988 dedication of the Dolores Hope Library at the school. Bob was then 86 years old. He told this story:

"There are five stages of senility. The first is when you forget names. The second stage is when you forget faces. The third stage is when you forget to zip up. The fourth stage is when you forget to zip down. I'm now in the fifth stage, but I forget what it is."

WHAT IF HE HAD SLICED?

Alan Shepard, America's first astronaut in space who later landed on the moon, also attended the Hope event. He and I have been friends since the 1950s. It was a beautiful, clear night with a full moon. I mentioned that it must be a great experience to look at the moon and know that he walked on it and performed all the things he did there.

He admitted it was a special feeling and then said, "Do you see the right eye of the man in the moon? Can you see the bright spot under that eye? Well, that's where I landed." The conversation then turned to his famous moon golf shots. He said he carried a fold-up golf club and two golf balls, with Houston Control's permission, but he was not to hit the balls unless Houston granted its approval first—providing everything else went smoothly. Otherwise, the public might criticize NASA for appearing to be playing instead of tending to serious business. He said he received the permission just before entering the module to return to the spacecraft, then in orbit around the moon.

I asked whether he had retrieved the balls to bring back with him, since they would be such unusual and valuable mementos. He laughed and said, "Heck no. The gravity on the moon is so much less than Earth's that those balls traveled six times farther than they would here. The last time I saw them they were going into orbit!"

LOSING WEIGHT THE HARD WAY

You can learn a lot about science in a few minutes, I found out. Alan Shepard and I had a mutual friend, Ollie Crawford, who was with Texas Pulp & Paper Company at the time. His firm had a large acreage of leased ranch land about 40 miles from Laredo near Bruni, Texas, for hunting and fishing. There were cooks, plenty of food, and Jeeps available for use by the company's invited guests.

On such invitation, several of us left Austin in a private plane which Alan Shepard was piloting. I remember this trip more for the flying than the hunting, because he kept demonstrating to us how it felt to become weightless in space flight. To do this, he began a descent to pick up speed, then maneuvered the aircraft into an outside loop. At the top of the loop we were momentarily in a weightless state.

After several demonstrations of this phenomenon, I told him I preferred to lose weight by eating less food.

A LIBERAL INTERPRETATION

My race for governor was over and I came in third, behind my friend and fellow Lubbockite, Preston Smith. Not long after I told Preston I would do whatever I could to support him in the runoff, I received an invitation to attend a fish fry sponsored by his supporters in Jasper, Texas.

They met me at the Jasper airport and we drove several miles by winding roads through the heavily forested Big Thicket country before arriving at a clearing where the cookout was being held. The food was good and beer was served to those wanting it, both during and after the meal. I made my speech of endorsement and encouraged my friends in that area to support Preston.

The editor of the newspaper in the small neighboring town of Kountz was a well-known liberal who disliked both Preston and me because of our conservative views. He spread the word among the news media later that beer was served there, which he said was illegal because it took place in a "dry" county. Queried about this by the press, I said I didn't know if it was dry or not because I wasn't quite sure where we were after making all those curves and turns through the forest.

The Kountz editor promptly wrote a front page story saying my remarks proved there was excess drinking there because, "Carr didn't even know what county he was in."

UP CLOSE AND PERSONAL

Jack West, who ran a 40,000 acre ranch near Falfurrias, was a good friend of Archie Pharr, past county judge of Duval County. The two went on a Wyoming elk hunting trip together and stopped to visit Yellowstone National Park on the way home.

Considerable publicity had evolved from an incident of a tourist being mauled by a bear earlier that year. That, plus the fact that it was winter, resulted in the two men being somewhat alone in the park.

Driving through the area they came upon a huge bear standing in the middle of the road. Jack approached the bear slowly and stopped the car with the motor running. The animal went to Archie's side and tried to climb on the car as Archie watched him through the window.

Archie and the bear studied each other through the glass barrier for some time, each seemingly mesmerized by the other. While this was going on, Jack pushed the control lever that lowered the window on Archie's side—but Archie was so intent watching the bear that he didn't notice the glass move and continued in rapt attention for several more seconds before it dawned on him.

When it did, he let out a scream as he jumped over, wrapped his arms around Jack's neck and jammed his foot on the accelerator. The car shot out from under the bear, leaving it sprawled on the pavement. Jack said that when he got the car stopped and Archie off his lap, he saw the bear sitting on the road looking at them as if to say, "What happened to those crazy S.O.B.s?"

He asked Archie later, "At what point did you realize your window was down?"

"When I smelled his breath," Archie sighed "and, let me tell you it was the worst breath I ever smelled on any bear!"

RIGHT TUNE, WRONG VERSE

The Federal District Judge in the Texas Valley was newly appointed and so was the bailiff. On the day of their first court appearance, local area citizens filled the courtroom to welcome their new judge to his duties.

The bailiff was nervous about performing his own ritual of opening the session with "Oh, ye . . . oh, ye . . . May God bless the United States of America and this Honorable Court," although he had spent a lot of time rehearsing it.

When the judge came out of his chamber ready to enter the courtroom, the bailiff was so excited that he yelled, "Here he comes . . . here he comes . . . God save America!"

EXCUSE ME, JUDGE

A trial in San Marcos required an examination of the jury panel to decide who the jurors would be. I was questioning a potential juror during this process when he asked if he could speak to the judge. We approached the bench with the opposing attorneys.

The man told the judge he had known me for a long time and had such tremendous respect for me that he would do whatever I asked him to, and therefore he could not be a fair juror. The court agreed and excused him.

I was walking toward the courthouse the next day and met the fellow on the street. I told him, "I appreciate the complimentary remarks you made to the judge, but I can't recall ever having met you."

"Oh, don't worry about that," he replied, "I've never met you before. I just wanted to get off jury duty."

I'LL DO WHATEVER YOU SAY!

My grandfather was elected Justice of the Peace in Commerce, Texas, and presided over trials in the back room of his general store there. One day I met retired Federal District Judge Joe Estes and he told me he grew up in Commerce and that my grandfather had greatly influenced him to study law. As a lad, Judge Estes attended many trials conducted by the elder Carr and remembered almost verbatim the defending attorney's winning argument in one of them.

It took place in the dead of winter on an especially cold day. The plaintiff was a landlord seeking eviction of a mother and her small children for unpaid rent. The defense lawyer's argument to the jury of six men went like this:

"Gentlemen of the Jury, you know what this cold-blooded landlord is trying to do. He is trying to get you to throw this little widow with her very small children out of the house and onto the cold street. You know how very cold it is outside this day. Most of you walked to this hearing room in that cold. This landlord wants you to throw these dear children and this helpless mother out into that cold. Now, I know you are not going to let this happen, are you?" pointing his finger at one of the jurors.

The juror at the end of the pointed finger apparently felt he should answer, and quickly replied, "Hell no, John, you know I'm not going to let him do that!"

THE DRINKS WERE ON THE HOUSE

Rudy Cisneros, owner of Cisco's Bakery, Restaurant, and Bar, is a legend in his own time. People come from far and wide to eat his Mexican food and to see and be seen in that popular place. When I first began eating there, I noticed he served liquor and other intoxicating beverages to his customers, who included just about everybody who was anybody in Austin, but he had no liquor license.

"Rudy," I said to him one day, "you have a lot of important people eating and drinking here and you're bound to get raided sometime. Think of all the embarrassment this could cause your customers." He admitted he should have a license and asked if I could help him get one. Soon we had filed application with the Texas Alcoholic Beverage Commission.

It was customary, upon receipt of such application, for the Commission's inspectors to go to visit the premises and determine if it met the requirements of the law. The next time I was at the restaurant I asked him how things went at the inspection. "Oh fine," he answered, "everything went just right. I gave them a drink on the house."

I almost choked, "You what? Good gosh, Rudy, you served the Liquor Board Inspectors an illegal drink? You could have been arrested!"

"Well, they seemed to enjoy it," he said defensively. "Anyhow, I got my license."

MAN MAY FLY IN THE NEXT LIFE

Having experienced more than my share of aviation near mishaps during my military and political flying, I needed no encouragement to become a member of the MAN WILL NEVER FLY SOCIETY. Its headquarters and meeting place was at Rudy Cisneros' bakery and restaurant.

Among the notables we invited as guest speaker, before we stopped having meetings, was local Congressman Jake Pickle. We asked him questions such as, "Will you please explain how a pickle flies?" Or, an even greater dilemma, "Why is Congress continuing to allocate funds to build airports when flying is not here to stay?"

Our motto was: "The Wrights were wrong."
Our tenet was: "Given a choice, we will never fly;
Given no choice, we will never fly sober."

These are still displayed on Rudy's wall and somebody ought to initiate the club meetings again.

WRONG NUMBER

It was my first trip to Memphis, Tennessee, where I attended a business meeting until almost 10 p.m. After the meeting, I was driving my rental car on the way back to my hotel and stopped at a signal light. Another car rolled up beside me waiting for the light to change and I noticed he was talking on a relatively new gadget—a mobile phone.

When he saw that I was staring at him, he lowered his window and, pretending he was passing the handset to me, said with a straight face, "It's for you!"

THE BIRDS DROPPED IN

It has been my good fortune to try cases in many courthouses around the State of Texas. Some of these are quite old and historical, which added to my enjoyment of being there. An interesting experience of this nature took place at the Lee County Courthouse in Giddings, about 50 miles east of Austin.

The century-old red stone building had no air-conditioning and the courtroom layout was unique. The witness chair was directly in front of the judge's podium, its back to the judge at all times. The attorneys' tables were on each side of the witness chair, facing each other. The 12 jury chairs were arranged in a straight line facing the judge. Spectators sat behind the jury chairs, separated only by a railing. The balcony was half-moon shape, as in an opera or theater house.

The judge and local attorney on the other side chomped their chewing tobacco all during the trial and intermittently used the spittoon or a styrofoam cup to unburden their cud. Tall windows that opened to ventilate the room brought in the constant sounds of passing highway traffic, which occasionally drowned out the court proceedings when an 18-wheeler truck went by.

Those windows had one other hazard—birds. They flew in and out through the screenless openings and sometimes perched on the chandelier directly above the judge's head. Being such an obvious "target" made him quite nervous and required frequent recesses while he called for the bailiff to, "Come up and get this damned bird out of the courtroom!"

THEY COULDN'T HIT MY FAST BALL

Most boys and a lot of grown-up men dream of standing on a major league pitchers mound before a large crowd and zinging a fast ball over the plate. My boyhood wish came true later in life—although not exactly the way I imagined.

The mayor of Houston designated one day in 1983 as American Legion Day and dedicated the baseball game between the Houston Astros and St. Louis Cardinals to the Legionnaires. As Texas American Legion Commander, I accepted the mayor's presentation and made a few remarks to the large crowd in the Astrodome. At the end of the ceremony, they asked me to throw out the first ball.

An Astro official handed me a new baseball and urged me to do it quickly because the Astros had taken the field ready to start the game. I asked where I should stand and he said I could merely hand the ball to the catcher or go out a little farther and toss it to him. If I really felt strong I could get on the mound and wing it in like a pro, he said in jest. Of course, I chose that option!

While Astro pitcher Joe Niekro held my coat, I turned to face the catcher and couldn't believe how far it was to the plate. All of a sudden I realized I might make a complete fool of myself in front of thousands of cheering fans, but by then it was too late. Summoning every ounce of strength, I threw the ball. The crowed reacted with mixed applause and I got off the field as quickly as possible without running. The catcher handed me the ball for a souvenir.

They later told me they had clocked my delivery at 45 miles per hour (about half the speed of a major leaguer) and called my pitch "unusual—sort of a curve drop roller." It dropped to the ground about 15 feet in front of the batter's box plate and rolled to home plate.

SNAKING AND SHAKING

To me, there is nothing like our vacation house in the Hill Country for peace and quiet, hunting, fishing, loafing, and searching for interesting rocks that Ernestine and I turn into jewelry and art objects. We bought this place on the Llano River several years ago and go there every chance we get.

We arrived one time just before sundown and I hurried to the water's edge to start fishing. The weather was beautiful and I enjoyed it so much that it was nightfall before I started back up the hill to the house.

It was then that I saw a beautiful rock glittering in the moonlight and stopped to pick it up. When I did so, I heard a rattlesnake just ahead and to one side. I jumped back startled, grabbed my flashlight, and aimed it in the direction of the snake . . . a BIG one. The light beam caused it to start moving toward some tall weeds so I ran to the house, loaded my shotgun, and hurried back to shoot that rascal.

More of a city boy than country, I was somewhat nervous approaching the dark area where I thought the snake was hiding and so cautious that I walked in a crouched position (as if that would make some difference to the snake). Then I saw what appeared to be a snake in almost the same spot as where I saw it the first time.

I held the flashlight above my head to keep the glare out of my eyes. I meant to pinpoint the critter with the light beam then quickly bring up my gun and blast it good, but the light cast a shadow on the ground by my right foot. It was the shadow of my gun barrel, but I thought it was that damned snake.

I don't remember exactly what happened or where I went flying off to, but when I regained my composure and returned to the scene, I found my shotgun on one side, my flashlight on the other and a large stick I thought was the snake in the middle of the road!

POOR LITTLE RICH GIRL

Anyone familiar with my area of the Llano River knows of its beautiful pink granite, quartz, flint, and other rocks. The area is also known to have cores of gold and silver from place to place—and an interesting history of searches for those valuable minerals.

I noted that much of the area of road in front of our house contained fine rock particles with a yellow-gold color, so I took a sample of that soil to Austin and had it professionally assayed. It revealed an 8/10th of an ounce of gold and 2 ounces of silver per ton. According to the assayer, that is more than some of the old gold mines in Africa were producing. It sounded great, but the outcroppings are not large enough for a profitable mining operation.

A couple of weeks after that, we had our 7-year-old granddaughter, Cherise, and her parents as our weekend guests. As she and I walked down the road together, Cherise noticed the hole where I dug the sample and asked what I thought might have made it and that the color looked like gold. I told her I made it and it did have gold in it. Then I explained to her about taking the soil into town and about the gold content.

She turned to me and said, "Granddad, you are a rich man!" then quickly added, "and I am so proud to be a member of this family."

OH, THAT'S WHAT I'M SUPPOSED TO SAY!

Tennessee Ernie Ford was one of the most unpretentious celebrities I ever met and a person I liked immediately. He was a fellow guest at a Confederate Air Force show in Harlingen and we had a good opportunity to visit together. I told him about our Llano River house and he said he had a similar place in Idaho, where he loved to go to relieve the stress and strain. He particularly liked the local people.

"I have one neighbor up there who is a judge," he explained, "and one day I told him, 'Judge, you don't look like a judge, you don't act like a judge, and you don't talk like a judge.'"

"The judge said, 'that's right, Ernie, I'm not much of a judge. You see, there are so few lawyers up here that we each take our turn on the bench. When my turn came, I didn't have any courtroom experience at all and I didn't know how to conduct myself.

"Then, after my first year, I went to a seminar where I learned that when a lawyer stands up to object to something, I'm supposed to say overruled or sustained.

"Until then, I'd just been saying, 'Bullshit, sit down.'"

HOMETOWN TREAT

Long after my days in the Texas House, members of the Lubbock Chamber of Commerce came to Austin to host a party for the Legislators then in session and I was invited. They held it in one of the local hotels and a large crowd was present. Part of the program included drawing names of the attendees to receive special prizes. The quality of these gifts impressed me, such as a weekend for two in New Orleans, and I was elated to hear my own name called towards the end of the drawing.

Approaching the podium, I contemplated receiving something extraordinary . . . and to someone other than me it probably would have been! However, Lubbock had been my home town for 20 years before we moved to Austin, and my prize turned out to be: my own personal use of a Lubbock city bus anywhere within the city limits for four hours!

★ ★ ★

THE LORD WORKS IN MYSTERIOUS WAYS

Many times during my courtroom experience I observed that one should never underestimate the power of the truth, especially when it comes from witnesses who lead simple and uncomplicated lives. This was demonstrated during a trial I defended in Victoria, Texas, in the 1980s.

My clients were a couple in their late 60's who, together with their son, were the defendants. The plaintiff was a local bank trying to foreclose on the family's small farm that was security for a $300,000 note. The defense against the note was a series of misconducts against the bank in securing the land as collateral.

The bank's attorney from Houston was self-assured and somewhat intimidating to the small town defendant. During the course of the trial, he cross-examined the wife in this manner:

Q: "Madam, you are suing this bank for damages, are you not?"

A: "Yes, sir."

Q: "And as part of those damages, you are asking for damages for mental anguish and distress?"

A: "Yes, sir."

Q: "Now as a matter of fact, madam, you have not worried about this case one minute, not one second, have you?"

A: "That's not right. My husband and I have been married almost 50 years and we have always gotten along very well. Now we are irritable, we have sleepless nights. I have developed stomach problems and it is very troublesome."

Q: "Now, madam, do you remember your deposition taken two months ago, at which time you were under oath to tell the truth, and I asked you that same question?"

A: "Yes, sir."

Q: "Well, madam, you were under oath to tell the truth then when you gave that deposition and you are under oath to tell the truth here today. Then you answered 'no.' Now, you say 'yes.' Will you please tell the members of the jury which time you lied?"

A: "I'll try," she replied, as she turned nervously toward the jury. Then she said in a quiet voice, "I am a very religious person. I read the Bible daily. I suppose I have read it from cover to cover three or four times. I believe what it tells me. One of the things it tells me is, 'Come unto Me all ye who are heavy laden and I will give you rest.' I believe that with all my heart, so when this gentleman filed the lawsuit and took my deposition and asked me that question, I said 'no I hadn't worried,' because, you see, when he filed that lawsuit I did what the Bible told me. I gave all my worries and problems to the Lord. It worked beautifully. I didn't worry a minute, not one second."

Throughout her testimony, she was on the verge of tears, unknowingly twisting her handkerchief into a tight ring around her index finger. She continued.

"Then, after he took that deposition, my husband told me, 'Honey, don't you realize the bank is trying to take away the family farm?' I didn't know that. The family farm is all we have left in this life. When I realized that, I reached up and took all of my problems back from the Lord. It has been pure hell ever since."

The jury's verdict said (in words I now translate as they might have been phrased in the Bible):

"Thou shalt not foreclose on the family farm;
Thou shalt not collect the $300,000 note;
Thou shalt pay $300,000 for the mental anguish that you have caused these fine folks."

NOT AS WELL KNOWN AS I THOUGHT

Texas - 13 was a statewide organization I headed in the mid-'80s with the objective to keep government spending down and taxes as low as possible. It was patterned somewhat after Proposition 13 in California.

Mr. Howard Jarvis had gained national recognition because of his leadership in getting Proposition 13 passed by California voters. Because of this, I invited Mr. Jarvis to come to Texas and appear with me at public meetings in eight Texas cities within a 5-day period. He flew to El Paso to begin our tour and after speaking there, we went to Midland.

Walking along the street toward the site of our meeting, I was amazed that ordinary citizens who had never seen nor met Mr. Jarvis in person, would stop to shake his hand and thank him for what he had done in behalf of the taxpayers of his state. I had been in Texas politics 14 years, with several statewide campaigns. Few people even recognized me, but they sure knew who Howard Jarvis was!

CAUGHT IN HIS OWN TRAP

Bert Wheeler of Houston, now Bryan, is a longtime close friend with whom I have hunted, fished, and made family visits to his exotic animal ranch near Hearne. He has earned the reputation of being a lovable character and his friends like to rib him about some of his antics.

A chance meeting with a local judge who knew Bert well resulted in his telling me this anecdote about our mutual friend:

"You know how Bert likes to invite these dudes from Houston to visit with him at the ranch. While they are there, he tells them all about the Indians who lived there back in the old days, their wars and battles, and so forth, and says they might find some arrowheads if they'd like to go out to a certain area of the ranch. Of course, Bert had already 'salted the mine' with these arrowheads, but the dudes didn't know that and they took them home and told their friends what a great place Bert has.

"Well, not long ago, Bert happened to be in Brownsville and ran across a garage sale where a man had a bushel load of arrowheads. Bert bought them for a song, carried them to the ranch, and spread them around as usual, so more guests could 'find' them.

"About that same time, some exploration company told Bert they'd like to drill some holes on his land to see if there were any coal deposits. Always looking for another dollar, Bert gave his permission. While drilling the test samples, the workers found some of Bert's arrowheads and took them back to Houston, where the headquarter environmentalist got interested and discovered they were from an Indian tribe never before known to have been north of the Brownsville area. The upshot was that the environmentalist prohibited any destruction of historical property, including any drilling for mineral samples.

"When Bert learned this, he got a little frantic at the thought of losing that income potential and admitted to the company the truth about the arrowheads. However, the environmentalist refused to be persuaded, because he thought Bert was lying just to make more money."

I saw Bert Wheeler later and he confirmed the story and added this brief sequel to it:

"During that time I had some of them dudes from Houston at the ranch together with some Englishmen. I told them all those Indian stories and suggested that they go look for some of those arrowheads that were probably lying around. Of course, I had salted the mine. I sat down under a tree to watch them.

"In a little while one of the dudes came up to me and said, 'Bert, those Indians could write pretty good, couldn't they?'

"I said, 'What do you mean?'

"He showed me an arrowhead he had just found with 39¢ written on it. I was caught red-handed and I made him promise not to tell the others."

Bert is a legend in his own time.

BLESS THAT HOLE

In March 1992, a young man from California visited my office and introduced himself as Jesse James IV —the great grandson of the infamous outlaw Jesse Woodson James.

He said he could document this relationship through family scrapbook items, letters, and his great grandfather's handwritten last will and testament. A California judge and others have claimed Jesse IV is an impostor and that they are the rightful heirs.

The modern Jesse said his great grandfather was 107 years old in 1951, when he died at Hood County,

Texas, under the alias of J. Frank Dalton. Legend has it that three bogus funerals were held during his lifetime and that he attended each service—even acting as his own pallbearer once . . . and that he was married 26 times.

Jesse IV and brother Woodson (Woodie) James formed a partnership with Australian treasure hunter brothers Darryl and Peter Fritz and a Mideast financier to recover some of Jesse I's buried treasure. They sought my legal advice on the partnership agreement and then asked me to serve as legal counsel and to defend them against other possible claims if they found the treasure.

According to the brothers, outlaw Jesse belonged to a Southern Masonic order whose members were outraged by Northern carpetbaggers' treatment of Southern people after the Civil War. The group set about amassing treasures by whatever means possible, converting much of it to gold bullion to finance a Civil War II. The brothers believe some of it is buried in Central Texas.

One such site is in Waco, near Interstate 35 on Highway 6 access road, behind the parking lot of an abandoned night club.

The brothers said their father, Jesse III, tried to retrieve a safe there in 1964 and actually raised it out of the ground, but it slipped out of the hoist clamshell and fell even deeper into the sludge below. Lacking proper equipment to relocate it, Jesse III called off the search.

Sometime in the 1970s, the owner of the property installed a 12-foot diameter steel casing down 36 feet into the same hole. His crew found the safe again and raised it above ground level for the second time—but, they, too, lost it in the muck before they could recover it.

When the partners started the 1992 Waco dig, I spent several days on site with them. The work area was ringed with security tape and guarded by Texas Rangers, so that only those involved had ready access.

Pile drivers set 40-foot steel caissons into the soil to provide a cofferdam 25 feet square around the existing steel casing, to prevent a cave-in during the digging operation. Each morning the crew pumped out as much as nine feet of water that had seeped in overnight from the nearby Brazos River.

The deep soil is a mixture of fine sand, pea gravel, and clay with somewhat of a quicksand effect. Water pressure from the river and digging vibrations cause it to move—making difficult any effort to locate an object.

Word about the treasure hunt attracted a small army of "sidewalk superintendents." Spectators milled around the parking lot observing every move made by the workmen, talking with participants and each other—mainly curious and speculative. Rumors ran rampant.

During one lull in the action, Byron Varner and I walked over to a pile of excavated dirt some distance from onlookers to hunt for interesting stones I might use in my jewelry making hobby. He was there at my invitation to see if he wanted to research the James story for a book. We picked up several rocks suitable for my purpose, pocketed them, and walked to the parking area to put them in my car trunk.

A bystander Byron had talked with earlier in the day approached and asked him in a half-whisper, "What were y'all picking up out there?" His face mirrored some doubt when Byron told him what we had found.

"Everybody out here was watching you two like a hawk," he countered. "They thought maybe you'd found some gold nuggets over there."

One fellow there said he was a "witcher." He carried an instrument about the size of a C-battery flashlight with a pointer antenna on one end. He claimed it was powered by radioactive material and could locate just about anything. When asked how it worked, he explained:

"I put a small amount of whatever I'm searching for inside the cylinder. When it is properly aligned with the same substance, the instrument reacts similar to a Geiger counter. For gold, I use a small nugget . . . for silver, an old dime. I can locate metal, water, human remains, you name it.

"To locate water, I put a vial of spring water in it and it works like a charm. You can't use city water 'cause it has too many chemicals in it.

"To find a human body, I load it with a sample of the proper blood type."

The "witcher" felt certain there was something valuable down there because, "when I loaded gold, turned it on, and aimed down that hole, I got a real strong signal!"

Jesse IV and Woodie said one of the keys to this location was a Masonic emblem on a headstone above a fake grave. It was in the Black cemetery across the street east of the dig site. We found the monument and saw the emblem on top of the stone. One end of the mason's square within the emblem was outlined heavier than the rest of it, forming a pointer to the treasure site. Woodie said the headstone was lying on the ground when they arrived and they set it upright, "so, it may not be exactly in its original spot."

Woodie said he remembered as a small boy watching his dad's efforts to raise the safe—in 1963 or 1964, he wasn't sure of the date—and of actually seeing one corner of the safe before it fell.

Darryl Fritz asked Woodie if he would submit to hypnotism to see if they could find out more specifics about that event. Woodie agreed. While under hypnosis, he remembered the date as May 8, 1964, and recalled the names of several other people who witnessed the operation that day . . . but when the doctor brought him out of it, he couldn't recall any of those details.

One of the many media people on site from time to time told of a brief conversation he had with a huge fellow sitting in a pickup truck.

The man told him, "They ain't gonna find no gold in that hole, I can tell you that!" When asked why, the large one replied, "They ain't gonna find gold cause I ain't blessed the hole, yet."

This self-appointed minister of a religious sect declared that when he "blessed" a hole, they always found what they were looking for. But he wouldn't bless this one, " 'cause they ain't asked me to, and I might not do it now if they did!"

The treasure hunt was still underway when the final edit of this manuscript went to the publisher, but two things are clear: If they find something of value, I may spend the rest of my life in court. If they don't find anything valuable, perhaps we should have asked that preacher to "bless that hole!"

ONCE UPON A TIME, YES

An attorney usually asks a lot more questions than he answers and I have asked a lot of them in my time. I also have been asked a few that made me stop and think. The one I remember best occurred in the elevator of an Austin office building and I'm still trying to figure out the right answer.

There was one other person in the elevator when I got on, a lady whom I didn't know. Out of the corner of my eye I could see she was intently studying my face. As I started to get off, she asked:

"Didn't you used to be Waggoner Carr?"

ABOUT THE AUTHOR

Byron Varner became interested in writing while serving in the U. S. Navy. As a Navy pilot in WW II and the Korean Conflict, his collateral duties in public relations and administration required written reports and frequent contributions to service newsletters. He later studied journalism and related courses that led to his eventual designation as navy public affairs officer.

For the last 13 years of his naval career, Varner served in a wide range of public affairs assignments that include opportunity for writing news and feature stories, radio and TV scripts, audio-visual presentations and speeches, and publishing newspapers and magazines. He also served as officer in charge of the Armed Forces radio and TV station in Guantanamo Bay, Cuba.

More interested in real people, true life adventure, and historical events than in fiction, this part-time author has written three other books and currently writes and publishes quarterly newsletters for national military associations.

Since 1971, Byron and wife Bonnie have resided at Lakeway, near Austin, where he has been active in business and civic affairs and occasionally writes articles for the community newspapers. One of his pet projects is the Lakeway Historical Society, which he helped establish in 1989.

INDEX

Regional Books From Wordware

100 Days in Texas: The Alamo Letters
by Wallace O. Chariton

The Battlefields of Texas
by Kevin R. Young and Dr. Stephen Hardin

**Classic Clint: The Laughs and Times
of Clint Murchison, Jr.**
by Dick Hitt

**Country Savvy: Survival Tips for Farmers,
Ranchers, and Cowboys**
by Reed Blackmon

Critter Chronicles
by Jim Dunlap

Dirty Dining: A Cookbook, and More, for Lovers
by Ginnie Siena Bivona

**Don't Throw Feathers at Chickens: A Collection of
Texas Political Humor**
by Charles Herring, Jr. and Walter Richter

Exploring the Alamo Legends
by Wallace O. Chariton

The Final Exam on Texas Trivia
by Wallace O. Chariton

The Great Texas Airship Mystery
by Wallace O. Chariton

Hardin's Pardon
by Dr. Stephen Hardin

Kingmakers
by John R. Knaggs

Rainy Days in Texas Funbook
by Wallace O. Chariton

Rattling Around in Texas
by Jim Dunlap

**Recovery: A Directory to Texas Substance Abuse
Treatment Facilities**
Edited by Linda Manning Miller

Regional Books From Wordware

The Rise and Fall of the Alamo
by Thomas Lindley

San Antonio Uncovered
by Mark Louis Rybczyk

Spirits of San Antonio and South Texas
by Docia Schultz Williams

Texas: An Owner's Manual
by Wallace O. Chariton

Texas Highway Humor
by Wallace O. Chariton

Texas Politics in My Rearview Mirror
by Waggoner Carr with Byron Varner

Texas Tales Your Teacher Never Told You
by Charles F. Eckhardt

Texas Wit and Wisdom
by Wallace O. Chariton

That Cat Won't Flush
by Wallace O. Chariton

That Old Overland Stagecoaching
by Eva Jolene Boyd

They Don't Have to Die
by Jim Dunlap

This Dog'll Hunt
by Wallace O. Chariton

To the Tyrants Never Yield
by Kevin R. Young

A Trail Rider's Guide to Texas
by Mary Elizabeth Sue Goldman

Unsolved Texas Mysteries
by Wallace O. Chariton